Early American
FURNITURE
FROM SETTLEMENT TO CITY

Early American FURNITURE
FROM SETTLEMENT TO CITY

Aspects of form, style and regional design from 1620 to 1830.

EDITED BY
MARY JEAN MADIGAN AND SUSAN COLGAN

An Art & Antiques Book

Edited by Mary Jean Madigan and Susan Colgan
Designed by Jerry Demoney
Production: Hector Campbell
Composed in ten point Caledonia

First published in 1983 in the United States by *Art & Antiques* Magazine,
a division of Billboard Publications, Inc.
1515 Broadway, New York, New York 10036

Art & Antiques: The American Magazine for Connoisseurs and Collectors
is a trademark of Billboard Publications, Inc.

Library of Congress Cataloging in Publication Data
Main entry under title:
Early American furniture, from settlement to city.
  "An Art & Antiques book."
  Bibliography: p.
  Includes index.
  1. Furniture, Early American. I. Madigan,
Mary Jean Smith. II. Colgan, Susan, 1946-
NK2406.E15 1983   749.214   83-2592
ISBN 0-8230-8007-2

Distributed in the United Kingdom by Phaidon Press Ltd., Littlegate
House, St. Ebbe's St., Oxford

1 2 3 4 5 6 7 8 9/87 86 85 84 83

Contents

Introduction

American furniture scholarship has come a long way since the late 1920's when such pioneering publications as Wallace Nutting's three-volume *Furniture Treasury* first undertook to document and classify the forms and styles of early pieces. Nutting and his contemporaries placed reliance on details of provenance provided by individual collectors, and on comparisons of dimension and stylistic detail that could be made by an astute observer with a tape measure.

Beginning in the 1950's, however, the researches of scholars trained primarily at Winterthur and affiliated with museums and collecting institutions throughout the United States have focused not just on stylistic comparisons, but on scientifically supported studies of constructional details and wood analyses, as well as on the examination of period documents such as wills, inventories, and records of taxation and shipping. Their findings have broadened our understanding of the influences that shaped early American furniture, the people who made and used it, and the extent to which it has reflected the changing values of the society that produced it.

The contributors to *Early American Furniture: Settlement to City* belong to this new generation of furniture scholars whose studies are rooted in systematic examination of both objects and period documents. Taken together, their writings, which have all been previously published as feature articles in the pages of *Art & Antiques* magazine, follow the evolution of American furniture from the first crude colonial settlements of the early 17th century to the sophisticated urban centers of the young American republic during the first years of the 19th century.

These chapters constitute a selective, rather than all-encompassing, presentation of early American furniture history. Many of them uphold revisionist points of view, based upon the scholarly researches of their authors. Virtually all of them emphasize the strong connections between furniture design and manufacture in Europe and America that persisted for more than two centuries.

During the years from 1620 to 1830, American furniture makers responded to design influences that were transmitted across the Atlantic in a variety of ways: through illustrated books, by examples of furniture "in the wood" imported by affluent Americans, and with the emigration of foreign-born craftsmen from furniture-making centers abroad. These influences found expression in the incredibly wide range of

The Dominy Woodworking Shop, which stood on Main Street in East Hampton, Long Island from the middle of the 18th century until just after World War II, has been reconstructed from architectural drawings for this installation at the Henry Francis du Pont Winterthur Museum in Delaware. Many generations of the Dominy family used these tools of the cabinetmaker's craft. In the foreground is a large wheel lathe; a foot-powered pole lathe is at the far end of the room. Workbenches hold such tools as a smoothing plane and an oak mitre box. A frame saw used for cutting veneer hangs from the ceiling; from the rafters at left hang templates for cutting cabriole legs, crest rails, and chair slats. Courtesy the Henry Francis du Pont Winterthur Museum.

styles and forms—some sophisticated and formal, others crude and countrified—that were adapted to America's specific regional needs.

Early in the 17th century, the first intrepid settlers to leave behind the relative security and comfort of England had, as their first priority in the new world, mere survival itself. Crude shelters had to be built, the land cleared and tilled, and provision made for security against hostile encroachments, before time and precious human resources could be turned to the manufacture of household goods. Reliance, in the interim, was placed in the meager store of objects brought from Europe. The first pieces of American-made furniture, as might be expected, were utilitarian; created by turners and joiners whose skills could be put, as well, to other useful purposes in the new settlements.

But European stylistic traditions had their inevitable impress even upon the earliest and most unassuming of chairs, tables, and case pieces. In his examination of the furniture of the 17th century New England colonies, for example, Robert Trent shows that turners and joiners tended to work in the styles typical of the regional English furniture-making centers where, as apprentices and journeymen, they had been trained. Despite the rich forest resources of the new world, many early New England pieces continued to be made according to medieval precepts of construction that used wood sparingly. Other, more elaborately decorated pieces of the so-called Pilgrim Century, Trent points out, derived from the design traditions of Mannerism that originated in late-15th century Italy, spread northward, and eventually were brought to England by Dutch craftsmen fleeing religious persecution.

In early Niew Amsterdam, as in the first New England colonies, pieces of furniture brought from Europe were vital elements in the transmission of style As Joseph T. Butler points out in his examination of the pre-revolutionary furniture of New York, such early Dutch settlers as the Van Cortlandts and the Phillipses brought with them furniture

in the lowlands baroque style, with heavy turnings, broad proportions, and decorative strapwork. He notes, however, that contrary to the assumptions of some early furniture historians, the English style had at least as much influence as the Dutch on 17th and early 18th century pieces in New York: so-called William and Mary, an English adaptation of lowlands design, is reflected in New York pieces of the late 17th century; and the English Palladian mode, with its simple architectural lines, was a strong element of New York furniture design through the first half of the 18th century.

Similar influences of William and Mary and Palladian design may be discerned in the furniture of Bermuda, which was a British crown colony and a major center of trade on trans-Atlantic routes. Betsy Kent notes that Bermuda furniture may be distinguished from its English and continental American counterparts largely by means of the native cedar from which it was made, and by such idiosyncratic details of craftsmanship as decorative dovetailing.

The importance of Palladianism to regional American furniture, no less than to formal American architecture, is reflected also in the unique raised-panel furniture made on Virginia's Eastern shore during the century after 1730. As Marilyn Melchor shows, William Salmon's house joiner's design book, *Palladio Londinensis* of 1734, was an important source for Eastern shore craftsmen who found in its plates the inspiration for raised-panel designs they incorporated into the cupboards, bookcases, and wardrobes commissioned by local settlers.

The persistence of certain forms that derived from European traditions of turning and joinery, but which were uniquely well-adapted to American colonial needs far beyond the period of first settlement, suggests a certain conservatism of taste and practicality of application that characterized much early regional furniture. The large wardrobe forms, or *kasten*, of the Hudson Valley and New Jersey Dutch settlers, and the *schranken* of their German Palatinate neighbors who settled

much of southern Pennsylvania, were inspired by late medieval European prototypes. Their usefulness as simple, commodious storage pieces that could be disassembled for mobility assured their popularity well into the first quarter of the 19th century.

Similarly, the so-called fiddleback chair—a turned form made throughout much of New York, New Jersey, and New England—derived from the early 18th century Queen Anne style chair with its graceful vase-shaped splat and curved back. But variations of this nearly ubiquitous chair, says Kathleen Eagen Johnson, were made well into the 19th century, and even reproduced during the "colonial revival" of the early 20th century.

While Americans favored utilitarian furniture, they placed a high premium on comfort, as well. In her study of early upholsterers, Wendy Cooper points out that theirs was a lucrative trade by the mid-18th century. The "materials used and the manner in which a sofa, settee or side chair is stuffed creates a distinct visual impression" that can sometimes "make the difference between great form and good proportions and indistinct and bulbous form."

Perhaps no individual has had a greater effect on the course of American furniture history than the Englishman Thomas Chippendale, whose 1754 book of engraved plates, *The Gentleman and Cabinetmaker's Director*, brought the curvilinear asymmetry of rococo design to American furniture making between 1755 and 1790. In the major cabinetmaking centers of Boston, Newport, Philadlephia and Charleston, craftsmen turned out graceful walnut and mahogany chairs, tables, and case pieces directly inspired by the high-style furniture illustrated in Chippendale's *Director*. By the mid-18th century, life in the major American towns was vastly more gracious than it had been a century earlier; landowners, merchants, and tradesmen of all sorts aspired to elegant homes and they provided a growing market for the sort of formal furniture Chippendale made fashionable.

Less sophisticated country craftsmen

interpreted the Chippendale mode to suit the needs and pocketbooks of their clientele, using local woods and adapting rococo ornamentation to the limited skills of local carvers. According to Marvin Schwartz, "ingenuity was substituted for elaboration; embellishments were trimmed down to preserve the spirit of the rococo while using a minimum of parts and a minimal amount of decoration; complex ornaments were applied in speedy ways; and carving was either simplified or omitted." For example, the Dunlap family of cabinetmakers dominated furniture production in New Hampshire, turning out sprightly and idiosyncratically ornamented furniture. Such pieces are today highly coveted as paramount examples of regional design.

A distinctly American type of furniture, the blockfront style, evolved in Boston during the Queen Anne period of the 1730's, but reached its apogee in the Chippendale period with the gracefully articulated block-and-shell furniture made by Newport's Goddard-Townsend group in the 1750's and early 1760's. Minor Myers traces the stylistic progression of blockfront design from Boston and Newport—where it began—through the small towns of the Connecticut Valley, whose cabinetmakers imposed their own interpretations on the style during the later decades of the 18th century.

Chippendale's influence extended even to the remote agrarian regions of the south. In the Georgia Piedmont, for example, Henry Greene shows that local variations of Chippendale design were created by itinerant furniture makers even after the turn of the 19th century, simultaneous with pieces made in the Hepplewhite mode.

By 1790, the United States of America was a fledgling but intensely prideful nation, newly independent of Britain, and revelling in its "government of the people," inspired by the classical democracy of ancient Greece. The nation's philosophic ties with ancient civilizations encouraged American furniture makers to adopt a new style of design based on classical precepts first propounded by the Scottish architect Robert Adam, and eventually translated into the cabinetmaker's vernacular by the Englishmen Thomas Sheraton and George Hepplewhite. Hepplewhite's book of furniture designs, *The Cabinetmaker and Upholsterer's Guide* of 1788, and Sheraton's *Cabinetmaker and Upholsterer's Drawing Book*, which appeared in four parts between 1791 and 1794, emphasized straight, tapering legs, lightness of form, and ornamentation inspired by classical motifs. As Victoria Brackenwhistle points out, plates in Sheraton's and Hepplewhite's design books served as the direct inspiration for documented pieces of furniture made in America during the last decade of the 18th century. In Boston, John and Thomas Seymour worked in the new classical style; and Samuel McIntire of Salem decorated furniture with carved motifs of classical inspiration, identical to those illustrated in Sheraton's and Hepplewhite's books.

The late 18th-century transition from Chippendale's graceful rococo style to the classic straight lines of Adam-inspired design occurred in the other decorative arts as well; it is most apparent in silver and other metalwares. The makers of decorative andirons, as Henry Kauffman notes, were quick to bring their products into line with prevailing fashions. Kauffman's survey of 18th and early 19th century fireplace furnishings reveals that Americans might pay as much for a fine pair of andirons as for a masterfully carved settee, attesting the importance of these implements in the early American household inventory.

In Baltimore, Hugh and John Finlay were among the best known furniture makers working in the classic Federal style inspired by Sheraton and Hepplewhite. They are particularly remembered for chairs and settees painted with commemorative and patriotic motifs, but as Ron Pilling observes, they had plenty of competition: there were at least fifty makers of so-called fancy furniture in Baltimore during the first two decades of the 19th century. (Painting as a means of decorating American furniture predated the Federal period by more than a century, however. Ruth Miller Fitzgibbons notes that the earliest painted examples were probably the simple chests made in the Connecticut River valley late in the 17th century; more sophisticated pieces of Japanned furniture, embellished with gilt as well as polychrome decoration, were being made in New York and Boston shortly after 1700.)

During the Federal period, New York City was a major commercial center, and a melting pot for many ethnic groups. Among the most notable furniture designers of early 19th century New York were Duncan Phyfe, a Scots emigrant; and Charles Honore Lannuier, who was born and trained in France. Phyfe is best known for his interpretation of English Regency designs, while Lannuier's urbane pier and card tables, rich with ormolu and marble, lent a flavor of French Empire design to New York's stylish parlors.

It was also during the years of the early 19th century that an American communal sect, the Shakers, established their enduring reputation as craftsmen of consummate skill. To the Shakers, utility and simplicity were the cardinal rules of furniture design; although later in the century, pieces they made for "outside" use reflected to some extent the prevailing tastes for ornamentation. The history of the Shaker movement in America, and its gradual accommodation to the secular culture, is reflected by stylistic changes in the chairs they made, according to Barbara Coeyman Hults.

In summary, as the various authors of this volume demonstrate, the furniture made in America from 1620 to 1830 is a surviving document of changing tastes and values as well as of American history as a whole. European influences are felt throughout the entire period, tempered by circumstance, availability of materials and skilled workmanship, and by local demand. In a survey as brief as this one, the interconnected threads of cause and effect can only be briefly illumined, but it is hoped that the studies gathered together in this book will whet the reader's appetite for further investigation.

Mary Jean Madigan

Early New England Joinery

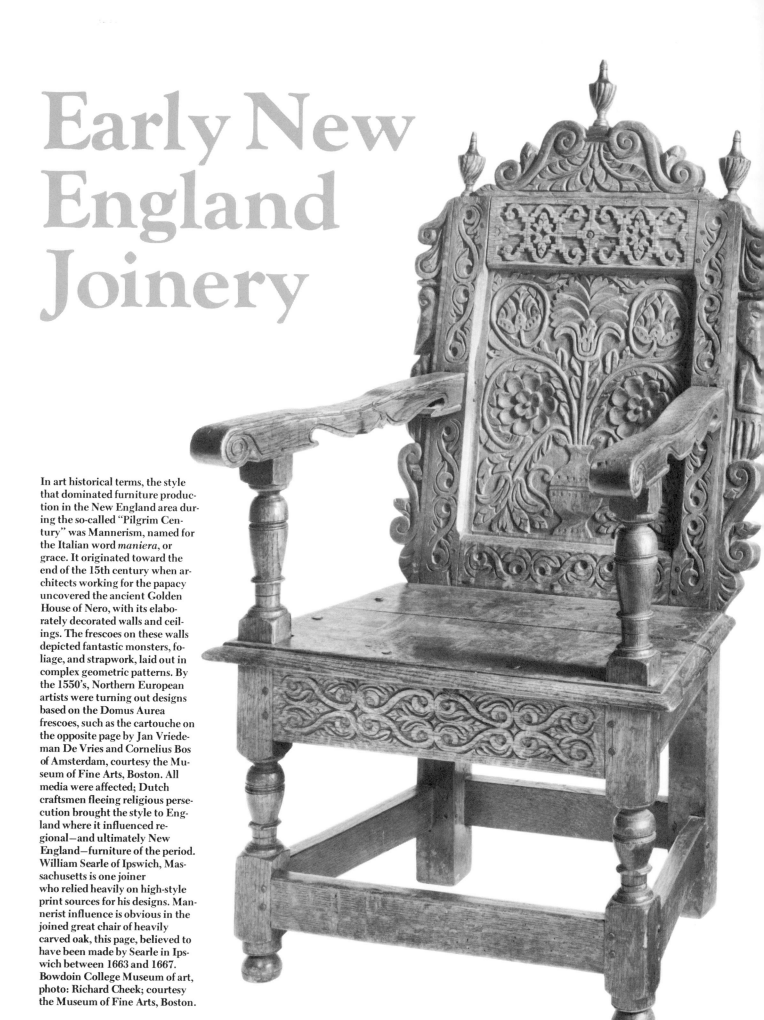

In art historical terms, the style that dominated furniture production in the New England area during the so-called "Pilgrim Century" was Mannerism, named for the Italian word *maniera*, or grace. It originated toward the end of the 15th century when architects working for the papacy uncovered the ancient Golden House of Nero, with its elaborately decorated walls and ceilings. The frescoes on these walls depicted fantastic monsters, foliage, and strapwork, laid out in complex geometric patterns. By the 1550's, Northern European artists were turning out designs based on the Domus Aurea frescoes, such as the cartouche on the opposite page by Jan Vriedeman De Vries and Cornelius Bos of Amsterdam, courtesy the Museum of Fine Arts, Boston. All media were affected; Dutch craftsmen fleeing religious persecution brought the style to England where it influenced regional—and ultimately New England—furniture of the period. William Searle of Ipswich, Massachusetts is one joiner who relied heavily on high-style print sources for his designs. Mannerist influence is obvious in the joined great chair of heavily carved oak, this page, believed to have been made by Searle in Ipswich between 1663 and 1667. Bowdoin College Museum of art, photo: Richard Cheek; courtesy the Museum of Fine Arts, Boston.

J oinery, turning and decoration of New England Furniture before 1700 was greatly influenced by regional English schools of furniture design.

BY ROBERT F. TRENT

In recent years, scholars have devoted considerable attention to the production of furniture in urban centers, particularly in Boston, but also Hartford and New Haven. Genealogical research and close study of English prototypes reveals that many London-trained furniture craftsmen were at work in these towns. The late Benno M. Forman ("The origins of the joined chest of drawers," *Nederlands Kunsthistorisch Jaarboek 31*, 1981) documented that two London joiners, Ralph Mason (1599–1678/79) and Henry Messinger (Boston 1641–1681), founded successful joinery shops in Boston. Each trained four sons in the trade, thereby

dominating the town's case furniture production. A London turner, Thomas Edsall (1588–1676), established a successful turning shop which flourished alongside the London joiners. As early as 1640, these workmen began producing high style case pieces with dovetailed drawers, often made in two parts so they could be moved up and down cramped staircases. Extensively decorated, these early case pieces often sport applied moldings and turned ornament made of exotic woods like palisander, cedrela, and lignum vitae from the Caribbean, as well as ebony from the East Indies.

London-trained joiners William Gibbons (New Haven 1640–1689) and William Russell (1612–1648/49), as shown by Patricia E. Kane in *Furniture of the New Haven Colony—The Seventeenth-Century Style* (New Haven: New Haven Colony Historical Society, 1973), settled in New Haven where

they made case pieces in the same London tradition, occasionally ornamented with light and dark walnut inlay, cedar moldings, and turned ornament.

The avant-garde style in which these Boston and New Haven examples were fashioned was attested by their advanced forms. The chest of drawers with doors, for example, was a form unknown in England outside London before the 1670s. It commonly has one or two cases with three or four drawers, concealed by wide doors ornamented with broad, projecting moldings. These same case pieces inspired the later and better-known "Dedham" chests of drawers, which often have the same molding profiles and architectural proportions. London-style joinery was a thing apart from the carved style practiced in most provincial parts of England and New England; its transfer to these shores at such an early date is remarkable.

Upholstered furniture constituted an important branch of the New England trade. Leverett couch at left, made in Boston of oak and maple ca 1698, is the only example with original covers. The Essex Institute, Salem, Massachusetts. Chair on page opposite, far right, was made in Salem 1685-95 when George Herrick was providing upholsterer's services there; turned ornament is attributed to Symonds shops of Salem. Oak, maple, and ash; serge upholstery is a new replacement. Museum of Fine Arts, Boston.

Boston's early turners

A second important branch of furniture production in Boston is represented by the work of turners. A large group of turned chairs with baluster or slat backs and magnificent urn-and-flame finials have not heretofore been identified as Boston products, because their histories of ownership cover much of the eastern Massachusetts and the Hartford area. No doubt these chairs represent a type made in Boston and Charlestown for export; it seems unlikely that Boston-trained apprentices would have dispersed from the capital to make these chairs in so many parts of the surrounding countryside. Only in Boston were turners able to mass-produce chair frames and ship them out.

Among the Boston turners working on a large scale were London-trained Thomas Edsall and his presumed apprentice, Nathaniel Adams (married 1652–died 1675). Testimony in a court case involving one of Edsall's runaway apprentices revealed that a good workman was expected to produce 120 chair frames in eight weeks. In Charlestown, across the Mystic River from Boston, a large family of turners was founded by Edward Larkin (Charlestown 1638–1651). Larkin's probate inventory referred to him as "Wheelmaker," but his shop included "Pump Tooles," "92 sive bottoms," and flaggs and Lumber," indicating that he was a turner and produced turner's wares. The probate inventory of Larkin's son John (1640–1677) is more informative, since it lists among other products a total of 320 completed chair frames. At the production rate cited in the Edsall court case mentioned above, this huge inventory must have taken five months to manufacture. Another Charlestown turner and shipwright, Stephen Fosdick (Charlestown 1635–1664), owned at his death a large shop with a wharf, timber and plank, half interest in a boat, and many tools. Fosdick also owned wood farms in nearby Malden and Woburn. Because urban woodworkers had to purchase all their lumber outside of their communities, they evidently acquired woodlots to secure a steady supply of raw materials.

Besides chairs, turners—especially in Boston—made other standard products. These included wooden dishes, platters, trenchers, taps or spigots for large wooden casks, spoons, flour seives strung with horsehair or fine cloth, spinning wheels for flax and wool, wooden shovels used to move grain in barns, bellows, and wooden pumps used to empty ship's bilges or great molasses casks.

It is not widely known that turners also made wickerware. Turners wove seats for their chair frames out of rushes, cattails, and thin strips of wood called bast, an aspect of their work which allied them with basketmakers. (London turners were introduced to wicker through the influence of Dutch turners who had come to the city as religious refugees in the 16th century.) It is therefore well within the realm of possibility that the famous Peregrine White cradle at Pilgrim Hall, traditionally thought to be a Dutch product brought over on the *Mayflower*, might have instead been made by a Boston turner. The shop inventory of Nathaniel Adams of Boston included, among

Left: Turned maple and ash rocker, 1650–1700, Boston or Charlestown. Ipwich Historical Society. The turners who produced this type of chair also wove seats for the frames out of rushes—as shown here—or of other types of material. Thus it was a logical step for them to begin producing other woven articles, such as Peregrine White's wicker cradle below, now in the collection of Pilgrim Hall at Plymouth, Massachusetts. The cradle, woven over an oak and maple frame between 1610 and 1680, was once thought to be Dutch, but new research reveals it may have been made by a Boston turner. The Pilgrim Society.

the other turner's products mentioned above, 63 wicker fans, three wicker baskets, and two wicker cradles. Adams died in 1677 of smallpox at the height of his career; there is no reason to think that he was marketing imported Dutch wicker, since his extremely detailed inventory would probably have listed that.

Upholsterers

Upholstered seating furniture constituted a third important branch of the Boston furniture trade. By the 1660s, upholsterers were able to make a living in Boston; It has been documented that ten worked in the town before 1700. By the 1670s, it seems likely that they were producing chairs for export on a large scale, for many examples attributed to Boston's upholsterers survive, with provenances over a wide geographic area. These chairs were covered in such materials as leather and Turkey work (a knotted pile fabric woven in England in imitation of oriental carpets), and in many different types of cloth. The covers were laid over foundations of linen webbing and sackcloth and marsh grass

stuffing. Four side chairs and an armchair survive with their foundations and leather covers intact.

The Endicott armchair is the only known New England example with arms. It descended in the Hart and Parsons families of Essex County, Massachusetts, with a traditional history of having first belonged to John Endicott, the Puritan governor of the Massachusetts Bay Colony. Research has revealed that the chair probably first belonged to the governor's son, Zerubbabel (1635–1683), a chirurgeon or physician of Salem. It was listed in his probate inventory among 4 great chayers" and "6 high Chayers." These high chairs were not for infants, but were high-backed upholstered side chairs. The Endicott example provides several clues to identifying the standard Boston product: a characteristic form of ball turning on its front stretcher and posts, heavy side stretchers that are rectangular in section, and a canted back with a separate upholstered panel. Unlike most examples, it has chamfered areas on the posts above the seat which are sheathed with

leather sleeves. The grass used to stuff the seat and back has been identified as spike-grass (*Distichlis spicata*), which grows in the drier sections of tidal marshes and was harvested for salt hay. As its name suggests, spike grass is dry and springy, and ideal upholstery material. Placed in the foundations of chairs, it was shaken and packed to produce the round-shouldered profile seen in early upholstered contours.

Turkey work survives intact on three Boston side chair frames and on the famed Leverett couch. The Leverett couch is the only example of its form in England or America to retain its Turkey work covers, and it too has been traced to its original owner, John Leverett (1662–1724), president of Harvard College from 1707 to his death. In 1697, Leverett married Margaret Berry, a wealthy widow of Boston. The probate inventory of her first husband, Thomas Berry, taken the year before her marriage to Leverett, listed "Turky Work for a Couch" among three sets of Turkey work chairs and other sumptuous furnishings. Undoubtedly, Leverett had a frame made for the couch

soon after he married Mrs. Berry, and the couch appeared in his own probate inventory among "12 Large Turky Chairs & Couch" valued at nine pounds. The couch then passed to Leverett's nephew, the Reverend Dr. Nathaniel Appleton (1693–1784), pastor of the Cambridge church, and was listed in Appleton's probate inventory as "A turkey wrought Settee." The couch was purchased from the estate of Appleton's son in Salem by the Rev. William Bentley and eventually was donated to the Essex Historical Society, whence it passed to the Essex Institute.

As important as its detailed provenance is the couch's superb state of preservation. Notches in the rear posts and hinges in the arms indicate that it originally had wings known as "falls," which could be raised to block drafts or lowered to serve as armrests. This extremely elevated feature is seen on many English couch frames. Remains of fringe outline the seat, back, and

arms. Made of red, yellow, and black woolen yarns to match the covers, the fringe was held in place by decorative brass nailing. The joiner and upholsterer in charge of making the couch frame to fit Leverett's Turkey work covers must have experienced some difficulty, for the upholsterer was forced to cut down the seat cover and to wrap a great deal of the back cover around the frame. The only other surviving Boston couch frame, at the Henry Francis du Pont Winterthur Museum, is about six inches longer than the Leverett couch; it would have been the exact size required for Leverett's covers.

Because almost all upholsterers worked exclusively in Boston before the 1720s, the existence of upholstered chair frames made in Salem is something of a surprise. One example whose turned ornament is attributed to Salem's Symonds family joinery shops was undoubtedly made in Salem between

1685 and 1695, when George Herrick was providing an upholsterer's services there. The frame differs from Boston examples in many respects. During restoration, inspection of the frame revealed a tacking pattern suggestive of cloth upholstery. (The frame has since been re-covered in green, twill-woven serge and matching silk fringe and galloon or tape, a treatment found in many probate inventories. Other materials used to cover chair frames included cottons and even silk brocades.) An extremely important and unique fragment of a New England-made upholstery covering, found on a Boston chair frame at the Wadsworth Atheneum during a recent restoration, is a plain woven wool cloth, now faded to a yellow color, which is block printed in a repeating floral pattern. New England supported many fulling mills where locally produced wool cloth was washed and pressed, and this example is perhaps typical of their products.

While many pieces of early New England furniture were stylistically influenced by Mannerism, still others reflect medieval precedents which continued in use because of their low cost or utility. The table above, constructed of a simple board and trestles, exemplifies this trend. Attributed to Benjamin Clark of Medfield, Massachusetts, it was made of maple and pine between 1690 and 1724. Similar in its utilitarian simplicity is the great chair at left, constructed of oak and maple in Plymouth County, Massachusetts between 1650 and 1720. Both, courtesy the Museum of Fine Arts, Boston. The massive chair at right, with its complex turned three-square frame and heavy superstructure, was made in Wales between 1550 and 1600 (five prototypes exist there) and brought to the New England colonies. It has served every president of Harvard College beginning with the Reverend Edward Holyoke, who held the post from 1737 until 1769. The turned ornament of the chair, as well as its heavy posts, is strictly medieval in form. The President and Fellows of Harvard College; photo courtesy the Museum of Fine Arts, Boston.

Heirlooms brought to New England

In the Victorian period, it was fashionable to claim that any example of 17th-century furniture with a family history had been brought to the New World from England by a distant ancestor, reflecting the belief that primitive conditions in early New England precluded fine furniture making. Modern scholarship proves that capable craftsmen worked here throughout the 17th century and that most examples said to have been brought from England actually were made here. But a few ob-

jects survive that were, in fact, made in England long before the colonists thought of leaving. Among them is the massive, bizarre chair with a complex frame and top-heavy superstructure that has served each president of Harvard University beginning with the Reverend Edward Holyoke (1689–1769), who held the post from 1737 until his death. Five similar English prototypes of this chair are known. It appears that the chair probably was made before 1600 in Wales and was brought to New England much later. Its turned ornament is strictly medieval in form as are the extremely heavy posts of which

it is constructed. Despite its thronelike appearance, the chair was in all likelihood made for use in a private residence.

Mannerism: a stylistic inspiration

Most histories of American furniture readily associate the Queen Anne style with the baroque, and the Chippendale style with the rococo, but no one has presented a stylistic basis for furniture made in New England during the 17th century. This furniture has been variously called "Pilgrim" or "Puritan" or "Medieval," but these terms are either

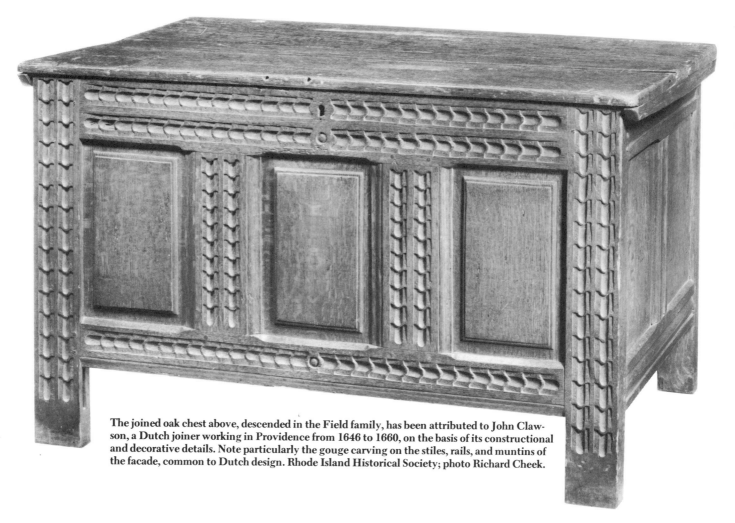

The joined oak chest above, descended in the Field family, has been attributed to John Clawson, a Dutch joiner working in Providence from 1646 to 1660, on the basis of its constructional and decorative details. Note particularly the gouge carving on the stiles, rails, and muntins of the facade, common to Dutch design. Rhode Island Historical Society; photo Richard Cheek.

incorrect or meaningless. In art historical terms, the style which dominated furniture production here was mannerism. Named for the Italian word *maniera*, or grace, the style originated in Rome between 1480 and 1500. At that time, architects and artists working for the papacy and for cardinals uncovered the ruins of the *Domus Aurea*, or Golden House of Nero, built after the great fire which destroyed Rome in 64 A.D. The walls and ceilings of the rooms, popularly called grottos or caves, were found to be covered with frescoes depicting fantastic monsters, foliage, and strapwork, laid out in complex geometric patterns. The subsequent introduction of this grotesque ornament into the artistic vocabulary of Italian artists marked a new departure from the formulas evolved during the early Renaissance, and the taste for grotesques spread all across Europe. By the 1550s, northern European artists were turning out hundreds of designs based on the *Domus Aurea* frescoes, which influenced designers in many

media. Dutch craftsmen who fled to England after 1560 as religious refugees brought the grotesques of the mannerist style to London and other major ports. Continental designs continued to influence architecture and furniture well into the 1660s.

The exact print sources for a number of New England schools of joinery have been isolated, notably that for the heavily carved furniture made by William Searle and Thomas Dennis of Ipswich, Massachusetts. The realization that Searle and Dennis were relying on high-style print sources for their designs makes their furniture seem far less folk-like than it has been considered in the past, opening up an entirely new way of interpreting all New England furniture of this period. Evidently, regional schools of New England furniture derived directly from the English regional furniture schools in which emigrant joiners had trained; these English schools, in turn, were influenced by major workshops staffed by continental craftsmen located in Lon-

don and other major urban centers.

Medieval survivals

While most 17th-century New England furniture was made in the mannerist style then fashionable in England, certain forms made here reflect medieval precedents which continued in use because of their low cost or utility. Most of these survival forms were roughly worked stools, chairs, workhorses, and settles made of waste timber like sticks, slabs, and boards. In Europe, this tradition of workmanship was a response to the shortage of timber and the relative poverty of the peasantry. Its continuation in heavily forested, prosperous New England was the result of innate conservatism. Such rare survivals as square-posted chairs with heavy slats, identical to those seen in many 17th-century Dutch genre paintings of tavern scenes, cannot be interpreted as evidence of a home made or frontier tradition. Certain aspects of their design, like the raked arms or tapered back posts, are influenced by high-style

The chest above was made in Plymouth, New Hampshire and dated 1685. Of oak and pine, it was probably made by a joiner trained in the West Country of Gloucestershire, where numerous chests with shield-shaped date panels and rondels surrounded by four leaf buds have been identified. Although the board sides of this example might be considered typical of the pragmatic American bent toward labor-saving, other Gloucestershire chests with this type of construction are known. Museum of Fine Arts, Boston.

joined armchairs. The significance of other medieval survivals, such as trestle tables, is more ambiguous. A recently discovered example, the Clark family table, was made by Benjamin Clark (1644–1724), a carpenter of Medfield, Massachusetts, from about 1690 to 1720. The table consists of two simple I-shaped trestles connected by a rail on which a third half-trestle is mounted. The top, made of two pine boards originally held together by cleats, rests on the frame with no connecting pegs or nails. This relatively light frame and top bears little relationship to the great, fixed trestle tables seen in manor houses in England, for it was intended to be dismantled and set aside when not in use. It bears a direct relationship to local architecture: a small house built by Benjamin Clark, now known as the "Peak House," still stands in Medfield; its beams are decorated with the same chamfers and lamb's-tongue and diamond stops seen on the trestle table frame. That rural farmers in Medfield were still using such an archaic furni-

ture form when their Boston contemporaries were purchasing long joined tables or the form today known as gate-leg tables suggests extreme conservatism in some areas.

Some regional discoveries

By tracing the family histories of major pieces of early New England furniture, regional joinery schools—characterized by construction quirks and carving styles—have been isolated. Furthermore, by investigating furniture craftsmen found listed in court records and probate inventories, it has been possible to attribute some objects to specific makers. Sometimes the English regional origins of certain carving styles have been isolated as well. The Field family chest, owned by the Rhode Island Historical Society since 1865, has now been attributed to John Clawson, a Dutch joiner working in Providence who was briefly involved in a witchcraft scandal. Clawson's chest reveals many features found in both Dutch and

English joinery, but a number of them are specific to Continental work. The panels in the chest's front have raised fields with molded edges, a detail common in Dutch furniture and in furniture made in New York City under Dutch influence. The rows of gouge carving seen on the stiles, rails, and muntins of the chest's facade are another common Dutch design. In an entirely different vein, a chest made in Portsmouth, New Hampshire, and dated 1685 was undoubtedly made by a joiner from the West Country county of Gloucestershire, where numerous chests with shield-shaped date panels and rondels surrounded by four leaf buds have been found. The board sides of this unusual example might have been considered an *American* labor-saving innovation, were it not for the existence of Gloucestershire chests with board sides and even board chests carved to look joined. Other Gloucestershire joiners were working in Plymouth County and in New Haven, where they made chests with this same style of carving. ∎

Pre-Revolutionary New York Pieces

Both English and Dutch styles influenced the furniture made in pre-Revolutionary New York.

BY JOSEPH T. BUTLER

Dutch influence on New York furniture of the late 17th and early 18th centuries has been widely recognized since Joseph Downs first observed in his pioneering work *American Furniture: The Queen Anne and Chippendale Periods* (The Macmillan Company, 1952) that "in New York the Dutch character of a century earlier lingers in the broadly built wardrobes and desks, deeply curved gaming tables and wide-seated chairs." This stoutness, along with a heavily proportioned cabriole leg, he attributed to the earthy influence of the commercial Dutch. But such an interpretation now seems simplistic. Early New York furniture forms, in fact, reflect not only the direct influence of Dutch—or Lowlands—style, but also two other influences: English derivatives of that style during the period of William and Mary, as well as English furniture in the Palladian mode that developed under George I and II from 1714 to 1760.

Imported Dutch furniture

Imported Lowlands furniture existed in New York during the 17th century—a small documented group of such pieces survives. The Dutch draw-top table that Frederick Philipse and his second wife, Catharine Van Cortlandt Dervall, gave to the church on their Hudson River-manor after their marriage in 1692 still belongs to the church. Its strapwork brackets and heavy, bulbous, turned legs are based on the designs of the famous Flemish 16th-century designer Vredeman de Vries. An imported kas—Dutch cupboard—in The

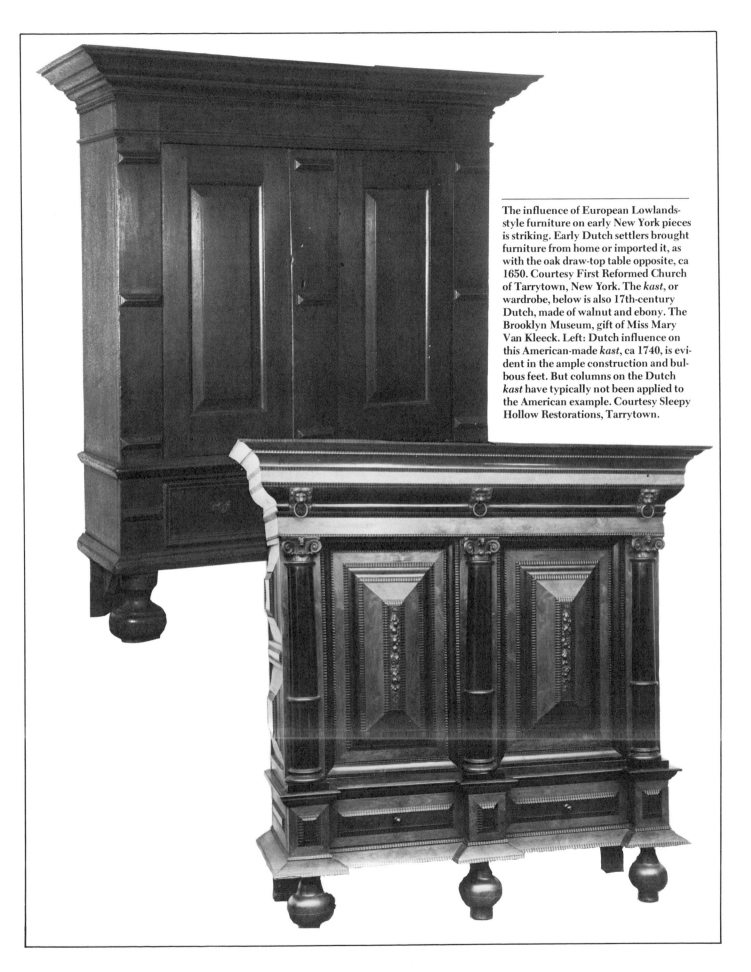

The influence of European Lowlands-style furniture on early New York pieces is striking. Early Dutch settlers brought furniture from home or imported it, as with the oak draw-top table opposite, ca 1650. Courtesy First Reformed Church of Tarrytown, New York. The *kast*, or wardrobe, below is also 17th-century Dutch, made of walnut and ebony. The Brooklyn Museum, gift of Miss Mary Van Kleeck. Left: Dutch influence on this American-made *kast*, ca 1740, is evident in the ample construction and bulbous feet. But columns on the Dutch *kast* have typically not been applied to the American example. Courtesy Sleepy Hollow Restorations, Tarrytown.

Brooklyn Museum collection is believed to have come from the 17th-century New York Baltus or Rombout families. The cupboard came to the museum through the Baltuses. Rombout, who was mayor in 1679, owned a "Holland cubbert." This kast of highly prized ebony and rosewood is ornamented with full classical columns and rippled moldings and is of fully developed Baroque form. Kasten such as this one generally lift apart into four separate pieces and are supported on bulbous, turned feet. Still another piece of imported furniture that is said to have been in America in the 17th century is a Dutch marquetry-inlaid tall case clock that dates from about 1680. It belonged to Francis Rombout, who died in 1691, and is preserved in the Madam Brett Homestead in Beacon, New York. Catheryna Brett was Rombout's daughter, and the Rombout/Baltus kast was also at one time in this house.

Dutch influence on 17th-century New York

Kasten continued to be made throughout the 18th century for those with conservative taste. Their form provides interesting proof of the persistence of a taste for Lowlands design even after the English takeover of New York in 1664. Columns on the face of kasten often were misunderstood by joiners in this country. They replaced columns or pilasters by simple "bosses," which are only reminiscent of a capital and base. The most decorative type of kast made during the first half of the 18th century was painted with grisaille designs—monochromatic paintings usually in shades of gray. These often took the form of pendant fruit and achieved a trompe l'oeil effect.

A New Brusnwick, New Jersey, cabinetmaking family—the Egertons—made the kast form through the end of the 18th century. Matthew, Sr. (died 1802) employed his son, Matthew, Jr. (died 1837) until about 1785, when the latter established his own shop. The Monmouth County Historical Society in New Jersey owns an Egerton piece which, on the basis of its label, dates from after 1790. A significant detail on this otherwise Baroque kast is its bracket feet, a form generally associated with the later Chippendale style.

From Holland to England to New York

English style, which itself reflected associations with the Dutch, also directly influenced 17th-century New York furniture. Lowlands taste of the late 16th century was extremely influential on English designers by the middle of the 17th century. This taste became fully developed in England under William and Mary (1689–1694). Two heirlooms of the Van Cortlandt family preserved at the Manor House, Croton-on-Hudson, New York, reflect this dual influence. A massive armchair made in New York about 1690 to 1700 combined turned members with carved C-shaped scrolls, leaves, and rosettes. The carved motifs are all derived from Lowlands design. The chair is ebonized maple, painted black to simulate the exotic wood that was so popular in Europe at the time.

The other Van Cortlandt piece that shows 17th-century English influence is a drop-leaf gateleg table. Its turned legs and four gates are in elongated baluster form. Made about 1700, the top is mahogany, the base cherry; the secondary wood is poplar. It survives as an early document of the use of mahogany in American furniture. The only other known piece from this same period that utilizes mahogany for a tabletop is at the Albany Institute of History and Art. The earliest identified owner of this piece is Sir William Johnson (1715–1774), and stylistically, from its shape and number of gates to the mate-

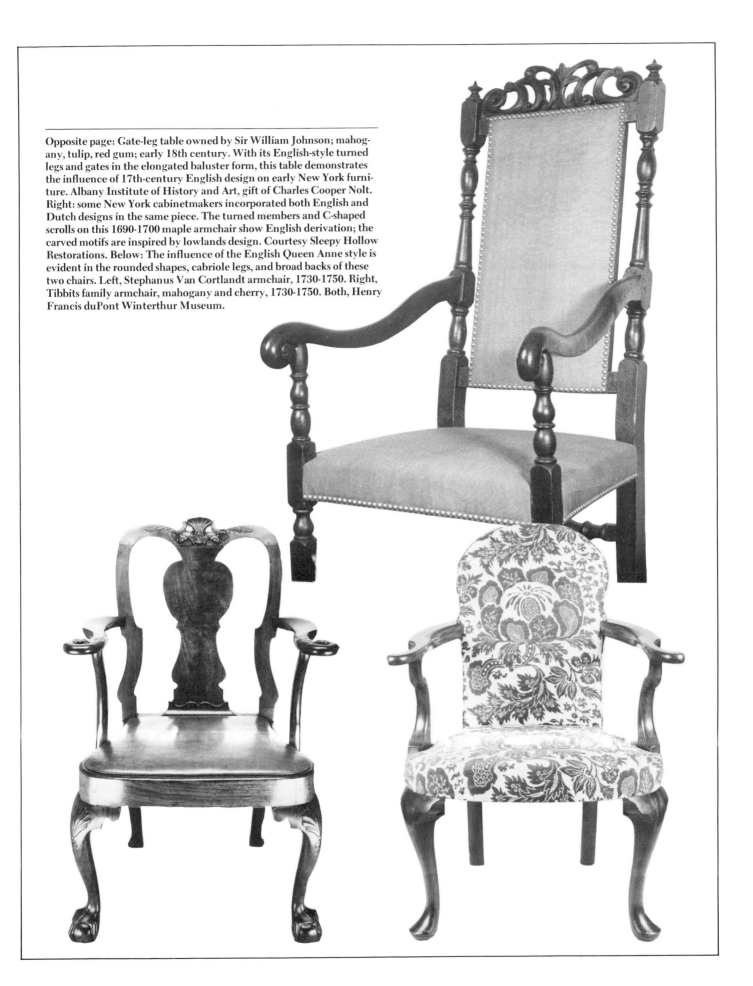

Opposite page: Gate-leg table owned by Sir William Johnson; mahogany, tulip, red gum; early 18th century. With its English-style turned legs and gates in the elongated baluster form, this table demonstrates the influence of 17th-century English design on early New York furniture. Albany Institute of History and Art, gift of Charles Cooper Nolt. Right: some New York cabinetmakers incorporated both English and Dutch designs in the same piece. The turned members and C-shaped scrolls on this 1690-1700 maple armchair show English derivation; the carved motifs are inspired by lowlands design. Courtesy Sleepy Hollow Restorations. Below: The influence of the English Queen Anne style is evident in the rounded shapes, cabriole legs, and broad backs of these two chairs. Left, Stephanus Van Cortlandt armchair, 1730-1750. Right, Tibbits family armchair, mahogany and cherry, 1730-1750. Both, Henry Francis duPont Winterthur Museum.

rial from which it was made, it is closely related to the Van Cortlandt example.

Because of the time it took for styles to cross the Atlantic from Europe, the Queen Anne style did not develop here until about 1725, and it continued in popularity until about 1755, or, roughly, throughout the reign of George II. This style represented the final phase of Baroque influence in England and relied on rounded shapes, C- and S-shaped scrolls, and the rounded cabriole leg. New York seat furniture in this style is relatively plain with emphatic curves and a pointed foot terminating the cabriole leg. By mid-century the claw-and-ball foot was adopted, and carving became more elaborate. Upholstered armchairs became popular. The broad back and seat and revers-

ing curves of a set of armchairs that belonged to the Tibbits family of New York are typical characteristics of New York Queen Anne furniture. Another important set of chairs was made for the Stephanus Van Cortlandt house in Manhattan. The cutout scallop shell and leaf carving in the cresting have a sculptural quality associated with the New York school. The eagle-head arm terminations are of the type that became popular in England during the George I period.

Just as the kast continued to be popular in New Jersey, on the north shore of Long Island, and in the Hudson River valley until the end of the 18th century, in the same conservative areas a type of joined chair was made from about 1725 to well into the 19th century. This chair form has a yoke-shaped cresting, vase-

shaped splat, turned trumpet legs, and pad feet. This type was painted or ebonized and through boldness of design often expressed the individual taste of the joiner who made it. As late as the first decade of the 19th century, this type of chair was advertised in Albany newspapers. A woodcut from the Albany *Gazette* advertising the chair manufactory of James Chestney illustrates one of these turned Queen Anne chairs that was something between a slat-back chair and a Windsor chair. In some instances such chairs were die-stamped with "D. Coutong" for the joiner David Coutant. The stamp is undoubtedly a misspelling on the part of the die maker. Coutant is listed in a directory as working in New York City between 1786 and 1794; he is listed as being in New Rochelle, Westchester

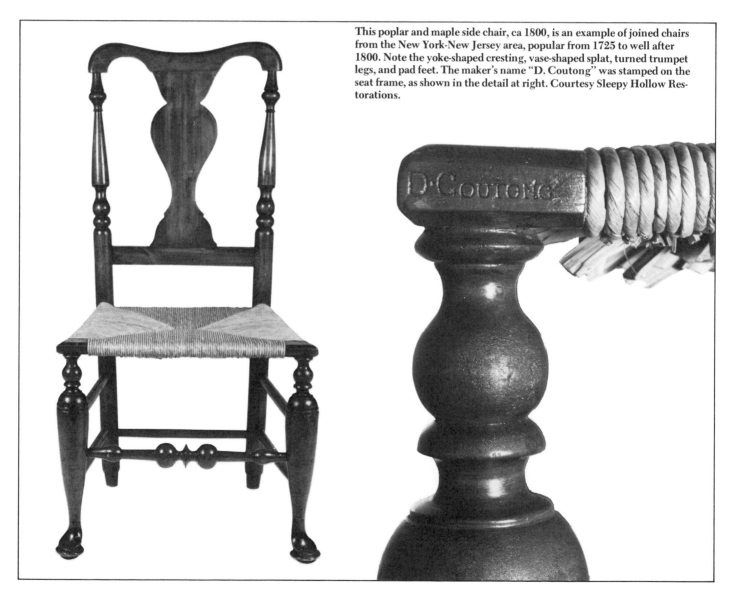

This poplar and maple side chair, ca 1800, is an example of joined chairs from the New York-New Jersey area, popular from 1725 to well after 1800. Note the yoke-shaped cresting, vase-shaped splat, turned trumpet legs, and pad feet. The maker's name "D. Coutong" was stamped on the seat frame, as shown in the detail at right. Courtesy Sleepy Hollow Restorations.

County, in 1800.

English Classical influence

In America the style generally called Chippendale became fashionable about 1755 and continued so until about 1785. While the influence of Thomas Chippendale's *Gentleman and Cabinetmaker's Director* (1754) on New York furniture was an important factor, there was a continuing conservative influence from the George I and II periods. In both England and America, during their reigns the full development of the Palladian or Classical taste took place. The buildings and written works of the great Italian Renaissance architect Andrea Palladio were carefully studied by architects and amateurs here and in England. Palladio had been a student of ancient Roman architecture,

and his buildings carefully reflected this influence. Palladian architecture embraced reason and rationality; the furniture created for such buildings reflected this philosophic approach. C- and S-shaped scrolls and the cabriole leg contributed to this sense of overall harmony. In addition, early Georgian furniture took on a more architectural quality. Case furniture was designed to be used in specific settings to enhance the architecture of a given room. The pediments of such pieces clearly showed their reliance on architecture. Classical details such as masks, exotic animals, festoons of leaves, gadrooned borders, and heavy animal-paw feet dominated the Palladian style.

By 1750 the succeeding rococo style was firmly established in England. More of a decorative than an archi-

tectural style, the rococo included the use of sinuous line, asymmetry, and delicate C and S scrolls when in the French taste. The style also embraced elements of Gothic and Chinese design, which were more popular in Europe than in America.

New York Chippendale furniture included elements of both the Palladian and rococo tastes. The Palladian taste is best seen in pieces of case furniture. A plain chest of drawers with chamfered corners cut with flutes and terminating in lambs' tongues reflects this style. Gadrooning, another Palladian design element, was carved at the base of desks whose exteriors are otherwise not ornamented.

A desk and bookcase attributed to the New York cabinetmaker Samuel Prince clearly demonstrates this archi-

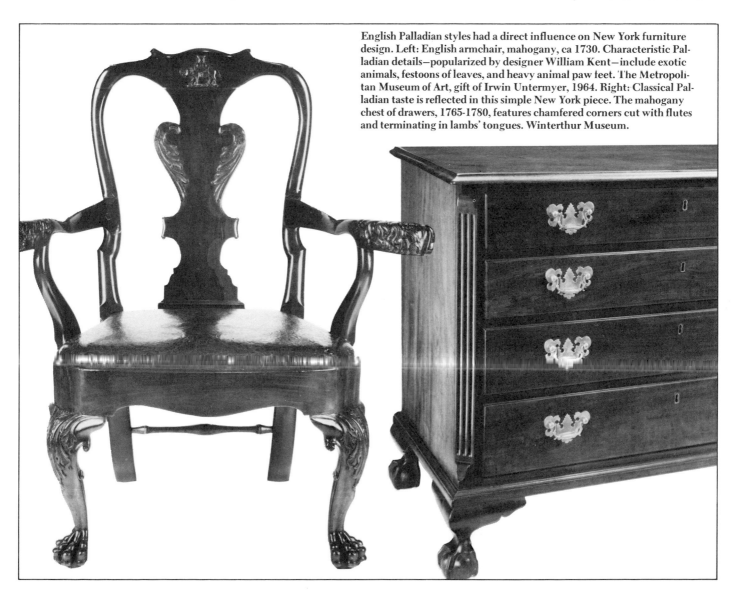

English Palladian styles had a direct influence on New York furniture design. Left: English armchair, mahogany, ca 1730. Characteristic Palladian details—popularized by designer William Kent—include exotic animals, festoons of leaves, and heavy animal paw feet. The Metropolitan Museum of Art, gift of Irwin Untermyer, 1964. Right: Classical Palladian taste is reflected in this simple New York piece. The mahogany chest of drawers, 1765-1780, features chamfered corners cut with flutes and terminating in lambs' tongues. Winterthur Museum.

The Palladian taste persisted in New York case furniture to the second half of the 18th century. Left: Desk and bookcase, attributed to Samuel Prince. Mahogany and tulip, 1770-1775. Note architectural details, such as the strong broken pediment. Right: Desk; mahogany, tulip, and brass; 1765-1780. Gadrooning on the skirt is characteristic of earlier English Palladian furniture. Both, Winterthur Museum.

Above: Many gaming tables were made in New York between 1760 and 1775. This example is crafted of mahogany, pine, and cherry. A concealed drawer behind the fifth or "fly" leg, but not visible here is typical of New York gaming tables. Winterthur Museum. Right: Chippendale-style mahogany side chair. Its tassel-and-ruffle splat identifies this chair as a "Van Rensselaer type," made for that family in the third quarter of the 18th century. Note the deep acanthus leaf carving, gadrooning, and squared claw-and-ball feet. Albany Institute of History and Art, gift of Emily Rankin and Edward Rankin in memory of their mother.

tectural taste. The broken pediment probably was designed to be in harmony with the interior architecture of a room that had an overmantel or window frames of similar detail. The urn that serves as a finial in this example is another direct classical influence. The diamond shape in the Chinese fretwork cornice is repeated in the pigeonholes, center door, and pierced brass pulls and escutcheon. Even pieces whose overall form is derivative of plates from Chippendale's *Director* reflect the more somber Palladian taste, such as a side chair with an interlaced figure-eight and diamond but little other decoration.

During the third quarter of the 18th century, New York cabinetmakers favored a chair splat carved with a tassel and ruffle, deep acanthus leaf carving, gadrooning, and squared claw-and-ball feet. Chairs with such decoration generally are called "Van Rensselaer type" because a set in this taste was made for Rensselaerswick, the family manor house near Albany. Another furniture form that is identified with New York in the period prior to the Revolution is the gaming table. It has a square top with indentations at each corner to hold candlesticks. The top is covered with felt and contains "ponds" for holding chips. A secret drawer in the back frame is generally found in such tables. Gadrooned and floral carved borders are often seen on such pieces. A considerable number of New York gaming tables survive today, proving the popularity of gaming in pre-Revolutionary New York.

New York furniture has never been as popular with collectors as the furniture from other pre-Revolutionary cabinetmaking centers such as Boston, Newport, or Philadelphia. It is probably the inherent restraint of this furniture that has contributed to this. Considerable research must still be done on this school of cabinetmaking. Such names as William Prince, Thomas Burling, and Gilbert Ash are identified as cabinetmakers, but more needs to be learned about their work.

To say that it is solely a Dutch influence that contributes broad proportions to New York Queen Anne and Chippendale furniture is not completely accurate. In reality, the blending of Lowlands Baroque design with Dutch-influenced English and English early Georgian Palladian design has created a unique type of colonial furniture. If New York furniture is approached as a combination of influences, its design is better understood. ■

The Upholsterer's Art

BY WENDY COOPER

From the late 17th century onward fabric and padding added immeasurably to the comfort and appeal of American furniture.

During the last few years, scholars and collectors have come to recognize the importance of superior form in upholstered objects and the value of surviving original upholstery materials both inside and out. The materials used and the manner in which a sofa, settee, or side chair is stuffed create a distinct visual impression. These factors sometimes can make the difference between great form and good proportions and indistinct, bulbous form. The fabrics used on the outside as the final covering are equally important, for they often emphasize the richness of the job, or possibly even the function or position the object may have had within the household. Leather, canvas work, rich silks, wools, and even simple linens were all among the possibilities from which an 18th-century client could choose, depending on fashion and the amount of money he wanted to spend.

Today we judge the merits of upholstered furniture by various standards that were probably neither of primary importance to the client who originally ordered the object nor even within his control. The epitome of quality today is sometimes seen in the vigorous sweep of the crest on a camelback sofa, sometimes in the proportions of a fine Philadelphia easy chair with generously shaped wings and arms that gently roll horizontally outward to gradually form

Original upholstery provides clues to construction techniques and common uses of early furniture. Opposite: Maple settee with turkey work upholstery, 1660-1680, probably Boston. Brilliant red, blue, and yellow wool was skillfully stitched over coarse canvas to imitate geometric patterns of hand-knotted Turkish carpets. The Essex Institute; photo Richard Cheek. Below it is a side chair, 1735-1765, Wethersfield, Connecticut. Cherry with pine slip seat frame and original needlework seat. Museum of Fine Arts, Boston, Above: Walnut easy chair, 1735-1765, Philadelphia. Sophisticated workmanship is evident in the C-scroll arms, generously canted back, and rare, shaped rear legs. Private collection.

a characteristic "C-scroll" vertically joining the side seat-rail. Or, on the other hand, to some collectors and museum curators, the finest quality upholstered objects can be distinguished by their carved or turned maple, walnut, or mahogany elements. A finely executed cabriole leg terminating in a strong, well-carved claw-and-ball foot, a meticulously cut Chinese or Gothic fret on a Marlborough leg, or a boldly turned medial stretcher on an early New England armchair frequently will make the difference between an object's being considered good, or great.

However, when we approach the subject of upholstered furniture from the point of view of the 18th-century client, we might find a very different awareness. For example, a rich and commodiously stuffed easy chair was usually more expensive than other pieces of furniture, owing to the high cost of imported textiles. The consumer purchased such a piece of furniture from an upholsterer rather than from a cabinetmaker. Until recent years, most American scholars have tended to overlook the fact that, as Brock W. Jobe notes, "during the 18th century the upholstery trade was deemed the most lucrative and prestigious craft profession."

The upholsterer's business was multifaceted, and today we might consider him a general contractor of sorts. By 18th-century definition, the term *upholsterer* was actually a corruption of the word *upholder*, and according to John Ash in *The New and Complete Dictionary of the English Language* (London, 1775) it referred to someone "who upholds; an undertaker, one who provided for funerals; one who makes beds and furniture for rooms, an upholsterer." In 1794 N. Bailey in *An Universal Etymological English Dictionary* defined an upholsterer as "a maker of bolsters" or "a tradesman dealing in chamber furniture." Hence, we can understand how someone who made bolsters and cushions might have come to be called an upholder, since bolsters and cushions were in a sense a means of support, though more important and more prevalent in past centuries than today.

A fuller description that gives signifi-

cant insight into the varied skills of the upholsterer in the 18th century can be found in *The London Tradesman*, a wonderful compendium written by Robert Campbell and published in London in 1747:

> I have just finished my House, and must now think of furnishing it with fashionable Furniture. The Upholder is chief Agent in this Case: He is the Man upon whose Judgment I rely in the Choice of Goods; and I suppose he has not only Judgment in Materials, but Taste in the Fashions, and Skill in the Workmanship. This Tradesman's Genius must be universal in every Branch of Furniture; though his proper Craft is to fit up Beds, Window-Curtains, Hangings, and to cover Chairs that have stuffed Bottoms: He was originally a Species of the Taylor; but, by degrees, has crept over his Head, and set up as a Connoisseur in every Article that belongs to a House. He employs Journeymen in his own proper Calling, Cabinet-makers, Glass-Grinders, Looking-Glass Frame-Carvers, Carvers for Chairs, Testers, and Posts of Bed, the Woolen Draper, the Mercer, the Linen-Draper, several Species of Smiths, and a vast many Tradesmen of the other mechanic Branches.

While upholsterers in colonial America probably did not exercise quite as full a range of duties as they did in England and continental Europe, they nevertheless did engage in a multitude of jobs including putting up and taking down beds, making bed hangings and curtains, paperhanging, and importing textiles and other small items of luxury and necessity.

Understandably, only a small amount of American seating furniture has survived with the original upholstery, yet these examples merit serious examination and discussion. In addition to studying original outer coverings, scholars today are beginning to take careful note of the construction of the furniture frames, as well as the materials and execution of the under-upholstery. Detailed upholsterers' bills, existing examples of original "stuff," and contemporary paintings and prints all contribute in this fascinating search for a more detailed understanding of the original appearance of upholstered American furniture.

In the 1929 Girl Scouts Loan Exhibition, the first to call attention to American decorative arts, several of the most extraordinary and remarkable examples of American upholstered furniture were shown. The Philadelphia Museum of Art lent its superbly carved easy chair, which is now attributed without doubt to the workshop of Benjamin Randolph, with the carving probably executed by Hercules Courtney. Today, this chair remains unsurpassed both in creation of form and in quality of carving. The hairy-paw feet, shaped rear legs, mask-carved front seat-rail, and carved arms seem exceedingly English in derivation, yet this need be expected since Randolph employed a number of the London-trained carvers, including Hercules Courtney and John Pollard. Furthermore, it was a most prestigious advertisement if a craftsman could claim to execute work in "the best London fashion."

As far as we know, the fully upholstered easy chair appears to have been nonexistent (except perhaps by importation) in the American Colonies before the 18th century. The earliest surviving examples of this form as interpreted by American craftsmen are a group of easy chairs with completely turned bases and slightly later ones with cabriole legs and Spanish feet. Unfortunately, none of the earliest easy chairs in the latter group has survived with original covering and upholstery. One has been recovered in a French loomed flame stitch that is not incompatible with the chair but most likely would not have been the type of material used with this style by an American upholsterer. Boston upholsterer Samuel Grant's accounts for easy chairs indicate that "cheney" was the fabric most often used by him between 1729 and 1735, with diminishing amounts of harrateen, plush, and "burdt" also employed. While cheyney and harrateen refer to woolen fabrics, plush probably would have been a silk pile-cut fabric and burdt perhaps a corruption of bourette, a fabric made of uneven silk yarns. Of course, it is also possible in this period that an industrious lady of the household, or a professional needle-worker, might have worked some canvas for her own easy chair and then had it applied by a competent upholsterer.

Brock Jobe's discovery in 1975 of the Thomas Fitch and Samuel Grant accounts has proved to be an important contribution to current knowledge about specific shop practices and upholstery techniques of 18th-century American "upholders," especially those in Boston. In most cases, the upholsterer supplied everything from the rough frame for the chair down to the binding and even materials for packing and shipping, if necessary. The account (in Samuel Grant's account book in the Massachusetts Historical Society) between Grant and Jacob and John Wendell, Boston merchants, on July 10, 1731, provides interesting insight into the entire finishing of an "Easie" chair.

Of course, Grant supplied frames for the chairs, and whether the client had very much to say about the style of frame and the material of the frame is impossible to determine, though Grant does mention occasionally that an easy chair frame had a "Walnutt foot." The girtweb would be the first thing applied to the frame, then a layer of canvas (actually linen) before the actual stuffing

Jacob and John Wendell Dr to Shop			3..15
2 Easie Chair frames	a	36/6	1...6..
Linnen 15/ Tax 11/			1..15..4
Girtweb 14/ Curld hair	8P	21/4	..17..
34 Yd. binding			4..18..0
14 Yd. Chainy	a	7/	....8..
2 Yd. Print			1..10
6P feath 1..1/ Tick 9/			3..12
line & thd 2/ makg 2 cha:70/			18..01..4
11 Yd rusha Linnon to pack in			....9..2
Truckg			....2..
			18..12..6

This page from the account book of Samuel Grant, a Boston "upholder," records transactions with Jacob and John Wendell, Boston Merchants, on July 10, 1731. It is a good documentation of the materials used to finish an "Easie Chair."

Facing page, upper left: Maple easy chair (secondary woods unexamined) made in Boston 1725-1735. Its upholstery is not original. Though its French flame stitch is stylistically compatible with the chair, it is not the type of material that an 18th century upholsterer would have used. Prentiss Collection, New Hampshire Historical Society. To its right is a mahogany easy chair with white oak, made in Benjamin Randolph's workshop and carved by Hercules Courtney between 1767 and 1777. Randolph employed a number of London-trained carvers in his Philadelphia shop, and attracted customers with furniture "in the best London fashion." English influence is seen in the hairy paw feet, shaped rear legs, mask-carved front seat rail, and carved arms of this superbly executed piece. The Philadelphia Museum of Art. Below the Randolph chair is a New York side chair, 1750-1760, of walnut, walnut veneer, and white pine with a maple seat frame. The needlework upholstery is original. Museum of Fine Arts, Boston. At the far left is Christian Gullager's 1789 portrait of *Mrs. Nicholas Salisbury* (oil/canvas, 35⅞" x 28¾"). She is seated in a chair finished with contour binding. Worcester Art Museum.

The chair at left, above, is perhaps the most extraordinary and well-known Queen Anne style easy chair still retaining its original upholstery. Made in Newport, Rhode Island in 1759, it was worked in crewel in full cognizance of the fact that it would be viewed primarily from the rear. The Metropolitan Museum of Art. Above, right, is a Windsor armchair made in New York in 1797. When a Windsor was intended to be upholstered, the seat was never fully shaped nor finished. This once-upholstered example bears the label of maker John De Witt and upholsterer William Gallatian. Colonial Williamsburg Foundation.

or "Curld hair" was put in place, and then it would be covered overall with more canvas (linen). the "Chainy" in the Wendell account was the finish fabric, but Grant also used "2 Yd Print," which probably went under the seat cushion, to save expenses where finer fabric would not be seen. The six pounds of feathers were for the cushions, which were covered with ticking and then finally the finish fabric. Each chair (and cushion) was then finished with the "binding" that outlined and emphasized the curved contours of the frame. A fine image of this important detail of finishing the chair with cord or binding can be seen in Christian Gullager's painting of *Mrs. Nicholas Salisbury*, 1789. Although Mrs. Salisbury is seated in a chair of somewhat later date than those Grant was making, the effect and importance of the binding is still the same.

In the Queen Anne and Chippendale styles, there are a few American easy chairs that have survived with either all their original upholstery and outer covering intact or with portions of their under-upholstery still extant. The Brooklyn Museum owns an important easy chair with all its original harrateen/moreen upholstery intact.

Unquestionably the most extraordinary and well-known Queen Anne-style easy chair of this type is the one owned by The Metropolitan Museum of Art. In terms of overall form, quality of cabinetry, proportion, and the remarkable workmanship and state of preservation of the canvas-work covering, this chair excels all others of its period and kind surviving to date. In typical New England manner, the great arms on this Rhode Island chair are formed by vertical, tapered cones that provide flat, horizontal surfaces for the sitter's arms

to rest upon. The cushion appears to be quite puffy, perhaps a full three or four pounds of feathers, and the whole is outlined with a narrow cord or piping. The marvelously colorful diamond pattern worked on a fine canvas covers the whole chair, with the exception of the back panel. Apparently the woman who created this fine handiwork realized that the chair would most frequently sit out in the room, away from any walls, and thus the back would be readily seen, so she worked a fascinating landscape in crewel for the back of the chair. It would seem that perhaps it was customary at the time to place a contrasting textile on the back of a richly upholstered easy chair, for a related Massachusetts example in the Bayou Bend Collection in Houston has a lovely flame-stitch canvas work on its front and sides, and an English harrateen or moreen covering the back. The

Above: This offer in *The Cabinet-maker's London Book of Prices*, 1796, shows that it was a standard option to have an easy chair fitted with a commode. Right: advertisement for upholsterer Richard Kip, ca 1771. Note the many jobs undertaken by the upholsterer Kip. The New York Public Library, Rare Books Division. Below: Plunkett Fleeson, a Philadelphia upholsterer, sent this bill to John Brown via the merchant John Relfe in 1764. It specifies the "parts and labor" costs of making an easy chair, as well as upholstering six side chairs. John Carter Brown Library, Brown University.

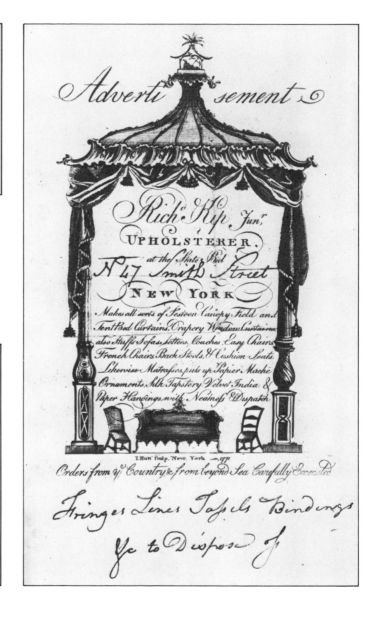

1764	To Plunket Fleeson D[ebto]r
April 13th	
To a Mahogany Easy Chair Frame	2:05:00
To Bottoming 6 Chairs @ 5/	1:10:10
To 11 Yds Harateen @ 4/	2:04:00
To 13 Yds Canvas for thee Chair @ 1/6	19:00
To 8 lbs. Curled Hair @ 1/10	14:00
To girth & Tax	07:00
To 3¹ of Feathers @ 3/	10:06
To 1¹ Yds of Ticken @ 3/6	05:03
To 18 Yds Silk Lace @ 8d	12:00
To Thread Silk & Cord	03:00
To a sett castors	08:00
To making the Easy Chair	1:15:00
	£11:13:11

Iook design is a rich, woven pattern of birds and butterflies.

When the upholstery was at one time removed from this superb easy chair, a signature was discovered on the back of the crest rail that read "Gardner junr/ Newport May/1758." While to date virtually nothing is known of any craftsman named Gardner working in Newport at that time, it is surmised that he was the upholsterer, since a Caleb Gardner, upholsterer, advertised in the *Providence Gazette* on May 31, 1783. Could the person working in 1758 have been the same upholsterer,

in upholstery or in chairs a father? Future research may tell us.

Frequently, easy chairs are associated with the infirm or aged, and they are often thought of as having been used in bedchambers. There is a large amount of truth in this belief, which is supported by paintings of the elderly seated in such chairs. Mrs. Salisbury, who was 85 years old when painted by Gullager, is an example. John Singleton Copley depicted Mrs. John Powell (1764) and Mrs. Anna Dummer (1764) in similar poses as older women seated in easy chairs. George Hepplewhite il-

lustrated a gouty stool along with his easy chair in *The Cabinet Maker and Upholsterer's Guide* (London, 1789) and stated that it "is particularly useful to the afflicted." In addition, one could have an easy chair fitted with a commode, as was a standard offer in *The Cabinet-makers' Philadelphia and London Book of Prices* (1796).

However, it is not unheard of to find an easy chair in a front parlor or a dining room as well as in a chamber. And certainly they were purchased by young persons as well as the old and sick. Both John and Nicholas Brown of

Providence, Rhode Island, were ordering easy chairs from Plunket Fleeson in Philadelphia in the early years of their marriages and again shortly after the births of their first children. Possibly this form was just as popular among nursing mothers as well as aging grandparents!

Rarely do we get any hint of critical comments from customers during the 18th century, but apparently Brown was not pleased with one of the chairs that Fleeson sent him in July 1763. In his next order he specifically complained, "Last you Sent us was Very Slightly made," and your suspicion is

Above: William and Mary armchair, 1700-1725, Boston. Superb carving and shaping distinguish this early oak and maple chair. The leather covering proved both durable and handsome, and the use of brassheaded accent nails was popular from colonial times through the early 19th century. The Henry Francis duPont Winterthur Museum. Top left: The legs of this 1765-1780 Philadelphia easy chair are in the Chippendale manner, with substantial claw-and-ball feet. In the course of recent preparations for reupholstery, the original 18th-century webbing, stuffing, and linen were discovered beneath several layers of 19th- and 20th-century fabrics. A fragment of crimson worsted, probably the original finish fabric, was found wedged against the frame. Private collection; photo Richard Cheek. Left: Armchair, 1793-1797, Philadelphia. Made of mahogany and ash by Adam Haines. This late-century French-style armchair is upholstered differently from earlier Chippendale or Queen Anne pieces. Its present state, stripped to the original upholstery and stuffing, reveals the upholsterer's technique of stuffing and building up the underpart of the overall form. When finally covered, such chairs were tacked along the edges with a single row of brass nails. Society for the Preservation of New England Antiquities; photo Richard Cheek.

that he is probably referring to the manner in which the chair was stuffed—probably not full enough for the corpulent frame of John Brown.

The overall form of a Philadelphia easy chair is different from that of a Rhode Island or Massachusetts one. Fine Philadelphia Queen Anne easy chairs are noted for the balance and grace of their C-scroll arms and more particularly the generous cant of the back. The feature of the shaped rear legs does occur more on English chairs, but a number of Philadelphia ones are also noted for this, including a pair now in the Winterthur collection. In overall contrast to the Rhode Island chair, the Philadelphia example most fully embodies a truly rococo spirit with its continuously curving outlines and aversion to any hint of stiffness and angularity.

A Philadelphia easy chair in a private collection has legs and feet executed in the Chippendale manner with substantial claw-and-ball feet and exquisitely carved leafage springing from the knee brackets and scrolling inward to trail down the knee almost to the base of the foot. One of the more fascinating aspects of this chair is that shortly after its recent acquisition it was discovered, as preparation was begun for its reupholstery, that underneath several layers of 20th- and late 19th-century fabric there still lurked the orignal 18th-century webbing, stuffing, and linen! Fortunately, the owner of the chair was sympathetic enough to the cause of scholarship to be persuaded to allow the chair to be studied and photographed in this half-stripped state before a new outer covering was placed on it for practical use. No obvious signs of the original finish fabric were immediately apparent when excess layers of fabric were slowly and cautiously peeled from the chair. However, as the job progressed, a small fragment of 18th-century crimson worsted fabric was found wedged against a vertical framing member. The final removal of all later fabric from the right-hand side of the chair revealed original linen, girt webbing, straw, and curled-hair stuffing. Furthermore, there was evidence of original brass tacks outlining the graceful curve of the wings and scrolled arms. With

19th-century padding removed, it was clear that the 18th-century upholsterer believed in a minimum of stuffing, placing it only for the client's comfort and providing a good definition of the overall form of the chair. One cannot help but wonder how many other 18th-century easy chairs might also still possess remnants of original under-upholstery.

This chair probably was made in the late 1760s or the 1770s and could have come from any of several prosperous shops in Philadelphia at that time. Certainly the carving is of the quality attributed to men like Hercules Courtney or John Pollard, but in the case of this chair the lack of any information prohibits us from trying to guess its genesis. We must also recognize that quite possibly a chair of quality could have been finished simply in canvas or linen and then fitted with a number of "cases" or slipcovers either to protect a perishable fabric that might have been secured to the frame, or simply to provide a change of color and pattern for the delight of the owner. As Nicholas B. Wainwright noted in *Colonial Grandeur in Philadelphia* (1964), John Cadwalader's accounts with Plunket Fleeson for 1770–1771 indicate that he had a number of sofas and chairs as well as at least one easy chair "Stuff'd & finished in Canvis" and with a case made to accompany the chair.

It is now believed that some chairs were never upholstered in a finished fabric but rather done neatly in canvas, and then a number of "cases" were prepared by an upholsterer. Certainly in Philadelphia slipcovers for chairs must have been quite exceptional, since Plunket Fleeson is recorded as having made quite a number of them for the chairs of John Cadwalader in 1770–1771. One portion of his account with Cadwalader noted charges "To making 6 chair cases red & white fringed thread & tape," and still again: "To 51 yds fine Saxon blue Fr Chk for Cases of 3 Sopha's & 76 Chair Cases/ To 152 yds of blue & white fringe for Chair & Sopha Cases." As can be seen in certain pictorial references to upholstered work as well as slipcovers, the use of fringe to ornament upholstery work in the 18th century was very much in fashion. Occasionally one of

these rare slipcovers surfaces, but few have survived intact; a particularly exceptional survival is in the Winterthur Museum collection and is made of English copperplate-printed cotton that is documented by Robert Jones, Old Ford, 1762. This chair case has a deep ruffle and narrow strings at the rear with which to fasten it to the rear stiles of the chair.

Unquestionably, the subject of upholstered American furniture is a vast and rapidly growing field of specialization. Scholars' interests range from the richly upholstered sofas and easy chairs, down to the less expensive, more common Windsor chairs, many of which had upholstered seats. A fascinating example of a once-upholstered Windsor armchair is now in the collection at Colonial Williamsburg, along with its mate and three Windsor side chairs. This chair bears the label of John De Witt (who worked at 47 Water Street in New York in 1796–1797). Over the maker's label is tacked that of the upholsterer, William Gallatian. Possibly Gallatian was buying chairs from De Witt, upholstering them, and then marketing them himself.

The technique of the 18th-century upholsterer, along with the chosen covering, meant everything as far as the finished, overall appearance was concerned. Recently recognized Philadelphia chairs bearing the label of Adam Haine are prime examples of this fact. Extremely French in style, the boxy shape of the under-upholstery is all-important to the overall of the finished chair. These chairs evidence in their original "stuffing" the skill and work necessary to achieve this important visual and esthetic aspect. While it has just been in the past five years or so that study in this area has intensified, a number of earlier scholars were insightful enough to recognize the value of original upholstery and to preserve it, as trustee Luke Vincent Lockwood did when arranging the purchase of an important side chair for The Brooklyn Museum in 1932. Future generations will benefit as collectors and scholars perpetuate this interest and sensitivity while they continue to discover, preserve, and study these important three-dimensional documents. ■

Chippendale: A Primer

T*homas Chippendale's designs inspired distinctive regional variations in 18th-century America.*

BY RICHARD DANA REESE

When Thomas Chippendale, fashionable cabinetmaker of St. Martin's Lane, London, published his book of furniture designs—*The Gentleman and Cabinetmaker's Director*—in 1754, he probably anticipated that both his reputation and his already sizable pocketbook would enlarge. He hardly could have imagined, however, that his handsome by-subscription book would eventually make "Chippendale" a household word, the synonym for a graceful rococo style of furniture produced in England and, from 1755 to 1790, in America.

Strictly speaking, Chippendale did not invent the style that bears his name. Illustrations in his *Director* (published in three editions dated 1754, 1755, and 1762) recorded furniture forms and ornamental devices already fashionable in London. By 1745 many cabinetmakers had abandoned the ponderously classical early Georgian style in

favor of the lighter, more playful lines of furniture in the "modern" French taste. This new Continental style (later called *rococo* after the French words for *rock* and *shell*, favored motifs) was curvilinear in form, with graceful S-curved "cabriole" legs. It was carved with asymmetrical organic decoration—"dripping vegetation," some have described it—brought into balance through skillful design.

The cabinetmakers, carvers, upholsterers, and "gentlemen" who purchased Chippendale's first *Director* found 160 illustrations of sinuously curved, extravagantly carved chairs, tables, beds, chests, and bookcases in the "modern" French taste. The chairs had ornately pierced splats, bow-shaped crest rails, and scrolled feet. The *Director* also pictured furniture in the medieval taste, then popular in England. "Gothick" chairs, having no resemblance to furniture of the Middle Ages, bore medieval architectural motifs such as pointed arches, trefoils, cusps, and tracery. The third edition of the *Director* included many additional pieces in the Chinese taste, as well. These had straight legs (sometimes called "Marlborough" legs), carved fretwork

stretchers, latticework ornament, and pierced pagoda-like motifs. Essentially romantic, the rococo or "modern" furniture was well suited to the exoticism of the medieval and Chinese decorative themes.

Chippendale in America

It is likely that all three editions of the *Director* found their way to America. The Philadelphia Library Company held a copy, and several prominent cabinetmakers in Philadelphia, Newport, and Boston may have subscribed as well. Besides the *Director*, however, a number of other contemporary English design books—by Robert Manwaring, Ince and Mayhew, and Thomas

Above: Philadelphia mahogany side chair, possibly Benjamin Randolph, 1760-1775. Until five identical pieces were found, this superbly carved chair was thought to be a sample, showing the cabinetmaker's skill. High relief carving, stump rear legs and paw feet are Philadelphia characteristics, as are side rails tenoned through the rear. The Henry Francis du Pont Winterthur Museum. Right: Mahogany chest-on-chest by John Cogswell of Boston, 1782. Bombé or kettle-shaped case furniture was made only in the Boston area. The Museum of Fine Arts, Boston, William Francis Warden Fund.

Boston-area cabinetmak-
ers were famous for
their bombé chests.

Next to the graceful pieces of Philadelphia, New York furniture appears heavy.

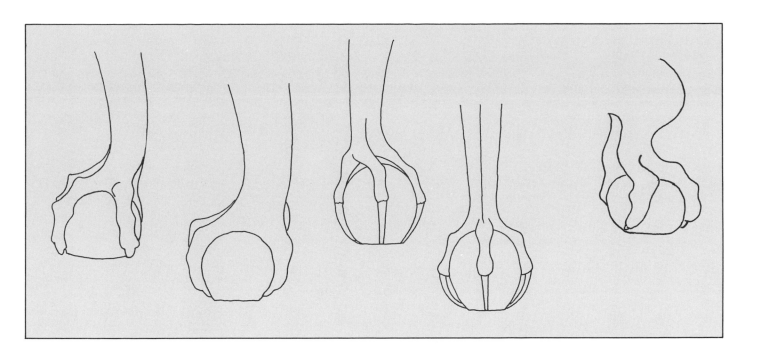

Johnson, among others—helped to popularize the new rococo style, which Americans did not call "Chippendale" until late in the 19th century. The emigration of cabinetmakers trained in English and Irish shops—possibly including several of Chippendale's own apprentices—also helped to spread the new fashion. And American travelers in England purchased furniture in "the modern taste" for shipment back home.

As interpreted by American craftsmen, the Chippendale style was more restrained than the highly elaborate designs pictured in the *Director*. A curvilinear style with cabriole legs—so-called Queen Anne—had been fashionable in the Colonies since 1725. Rococo ornamentation—carving of scrolls and foliate motifs, fretting, and pierced work was introduced to this basic form to create furniture in the new Chippendale taste. On chairs, vertical

stiles and a cupid's-bow–shaped crest rail, forming "ears" at their juncture, replaced the curved Queen Anne back. Claw-and-ball feet—out of fashion in England since 1750 and therefore not illustrated in the *Director*—supplanted the earlier pad. Other familiar furniture forms, including highboys (tall chests on legs) and tea tables, received new decorative treatment to conform with the Chippendale style.

As the coming of Chippendale coincided with a general improvement in the American standard of living, several new types of furniture evolved to accommodate the growing taste for luxury. The dropped-leaf—or "Pembroke"—breakfast table, pole firescreen, and a variety of small stands to hold kettles, basins, and lighting devices were innovations of what has come to be called the Chippendale era (1755–1790) in America. Large upholstered wing or "easy" chairs became more popular at this time. They were often covered with a heavy, patterned English worsted known as *harrateen* or *moreen*, dyed crimson, blue, green, or yellow. Moreen had a watered effect, achieved by stamping the wet cloth in wavy patterns with a hot iron.

By the mid-18th century nearly every major American center of trade had an established community of cabinetmakers. Within the larger towns of

Philadelphia, Boston, New York, and Newport, furniture craftsmen specialized. Working to order out of their own shops, turners—or latheworkers—produced stretchers, columns, finials, drops, and other elements. Skilled carvers created ornamentation (piercing, relief carving, fluting, gadrooning) and inlay work. Decorative painters and japanners worked with plaster, gilt, paint, and varnish to enliven the surfaces of finished furniture. The cabinetmaker or "joiner," who often employed a number of apprentices and journeymen, put all the parts together and received credit for the total result.

Eighteenth-century customers could order what they wanted in the way of wood and ornamentation for a piece of furniture, the final cost depending on the number of "options"—brackets moldings, fluted or carved decoration—chosen. Design books such as the *Director* inspired customers to select from among a number of fashionable forms and decorations. Thus the taste and pocketbook of the customer had at least as great an effect on the stylistic production of a given cabinetmaker as did the innate artistry of the joiner himself.

Intracoastal and Caribbean sea trade was important to Chippendale furniture manufacture. Santo Domingo and Honduras mahogany were widely imported to all the major cabinetmaking centers, especially those of Philadelphia and Charleston. Native southern black walnut and red cedar were shipped to northern ports, while great quantities of New England white pine went southward. Furniture from northern ports was sometimes shipped south as "venture cargo" (the ship's captain had leave to sell such wares for the best price he could get, stocking up on other goods before sailing on to the next port).

Regional characteristics of formal Chippendale furniture

Few American cabinetmakers signed their furniture during the Chippendale period, making identification tricky at best. On the basis of the few marked pieces and others whose descent through regional families has been well documented, furniture historians have established some general stylistic and constructional guidelines for identifying distinct "schools" of cabinetmaking in Philadelphia, New York, Boston, Newport, and the South.

The primary wood (used to construct the outer, visible parts) of a piece of furniture is not always a reliable indicator of regional origins, for such nonnative woods as mahogany were widely used. More dependable is an analysis of the "secondary" woods—those chosen to line drawers, brace chair corners, and so on. City cabinetmakers tended to favor secondary woods native to their regions and therefore cheaply obtained. (Country joiners used local wood for entire pieces of furniture.)

Methods of construction offer more positive clues. Under the apprenticeship system, schools of cabinetmakers passed traditional joining methods from father to son, master to apprentice. Each regional school had its preferred way to brace chair seats, dovetail drawers, and fit major elements. Stylistic features also differ from region to region. The shape of the ball-and-claw foot, for example, is a distinctive regional characteristic. Quality of carved work, variations in form and proportion, and the use of specific decorative motifs—shells, pinwheels, spiral finials—are further aids to regional

identification. Country furniture, though idiosyncratically proportioned and relatively crude in execution, usually reflected the stylistic and constructional preferences of nearby high-style schools of cabinetmakers.

The Philadelphia school

Larger than New York or Boston, Philadelphia was the foremost center of wealth, luxury, and gracious living in mid-19th century America. Despite its Quaker tradition of simplicity, Philadelphia society was stylish, providing a brisk market for elaborately fashionable furniture in the manner of Chippendale's *Director*. Cabinetmakers trained in the European centers—particularly London and Ireland—emigrated to Philadelphia, bringing a direct knowledge of the current English vogue. Santo Domingo and Honduras mahogany were imported in great quantity, encouraging a lavish use of this wood for entire pieces of furniture, inside as well as out.

Hallmarks of the Philadelphia style are its fine carving, of great depth and plasticity, and the exquisite proportion of its case pieces (chests, desks, highboys, and other furniture constructed over a case or frame). *Side chairs* usually have simply finished round back legs. These "stump" legs contrast with the front cabriole legs, which usually are carved in high relief at the knee and terminate in ball-and-claw, scrolled, or occasionally hairy paw feet. Philadelphia ball-and-claw feet have finely delineated knuckles, tightly grasping a somewhat flattened ball. (Hairy paw feet, shown in Chippendale's *Director*, are found in America only at Boston and Philadelphia, and then only rarely.) Treatment of chair splats varies from relatively simple piercing to the ornate tracery and fretwork of the Gothic or Chinese taste. The graceful ears of Philadelphia chairs are large and well developed. Fabric-covered slip seats—which literally slip into the shaped seat frame—are usual, although some chairs are upholstered over the seat rail. Seat rails are nearly always tenoned completely through the rear stiles, a visible construction technique typical of Philadelphia. (A tenon is a peg-like

projection fitted into a receiving cavity—or mortise—to join sections of furniture.) Inner seat frames are blocked for strength with quarter rounds of cedar or white tulipwood. Upholstered easy or *wing chairs* have horizontally positioned C-scrolled armrests, and no stretchers.

Noted for their fine proportion, Philadelphia highboys have scrolled, broken-pediment tops, centered by pierced cartouche or cabochon decorations (a cabochon is an asymmetrical convex shape, like a peanut) and flanked by distinctive flame-shaped finials. Colonnettes—quarter columns—sometimes fluted or carved with vines, frame the sides of many Philadelphia case pieces. *Tilt-top tables* have a rotating "bird cage" of elongated spindles under the top. They are distinguished by their urn-and-ball pedestals (the ball is slightly flattened), curved ankles that dip close to the floor, and superb high-relief carving.

William Savery was possibly the first Philadelphian to work in the Chippendale style. Savery was a Quaker whose furniture was relatively plain. He did not own carving tools. Benjamin Randolph, active from 1760 to 1790, made elegantly carved furniture in the manner of Chippendale's. He is linked to six so-called sample chairs thought to be unique, and noted for their extreme elegance and exquisite carving. (The "sample" theory suffered in 1974 when five chairs matching one of the samples

Opposite page: Breakfront bookcase, attributed to Thomas Elfe of Charleston, ca 1770. In America, the breakfront bookcase is a form unique to Charleston in the Chippendale period. This example closely approximates a design illustrated in Chippendale's *Director*, but was heightened to the spacious dimensions of Charleston rooms. Its delicately fretted top is typical of the work of Thomas Elfe, whose Charleston account books from 1768 to 1775 reveal he made several large fretted bookcases during that period. The elegance of this large piece of furniture testifies to Charleston's ambience of fashionable living in the British manner. Its American manufacture, however, is confirmed by the use of cypress as a secondary wood. (Cypress was native to the Charleston area.) The Museum of Early Southern Decorative Arts, Winston-Salem North Carolina.

Stylish Charleston furniture rivaled that of England's best cabinetmakers.

Above: Card Table of mahogany, cherry and pine, New York ca 1760-1775. New York gaming tables often have a hidden drawer behind the fifth or "fly" leg. The gadrooned skirt, knees carved in low relief, and blocky ball-and-claw feet are all typical of New York design. Above, right: Mahogany side chair by Daniel Trotter of Philadelphia, ca 1775-1800. Chairs with horizontal splats "knotted" in the middle are sometimes called "pretzel backs." These often have straight or Marlborough legs. Both pieces, Winterthur Museum.

came to light and were sold at Parke Bernet for over $200,000.) James Gillingham (1739–1781) is associated with chairs having pierced trefoils in the back splat. Daniel Trotter (1747–1800) made ladder-back Chippendale chairs—aptly called "pretzel-backs"—with straight Marlborough legs. Thomas Affleck, an English-trained Scot, came to Philadelphia about 1763. He owned a copy of the *Director*, which may have inspired his work in the fretted "Chinese Chippendale" style.

New York Chippendale

In contrast to the graceful pieces of Philadelphia, New York furniture appears squat and heavy, with broadly proportioned chair seats and backs. (New York in the mid-18th century was a very rough-and-tumble mercantile town, where utility and comfort counted for more than mere fashion.) In general the Chippendale style is inter-preted with great restraint in New York, where the most commonly made pieces of furniture at this time were tables and chairs. A holdover from the Queen Anne period, the *corner chair* or *roundabout* continued to be popular. The traditional solid splats of such chairs are pierced in the new fashion; their cabriole legs terminate in claw-and-ball feet. (The New York claw-and-ball is distinctively squared off—even blocklike—with the talons close to the ball.) Side chairs have a pierced splat of interlacing elements, centered by a characteristic "kite" or diamond shape that has been linked with the workshop of Gilbert Ash (1714–1785). Distinctive New York rear legs have a shaped, pointed platform foot that is often found on British chairs. Gadrooning (rufflelike carving) on the apron of New York chairs adds to their illusion of broadness. They are often underframed with diagonal strips, an English practice.

The five-legged *card table* that conceals a drawer behind the fifth or "fly" leg is a distinctively New York form. These gaming tables are usually serpentine (having sinuously shaped tops) and are gadroon carved across the aprons. Carving at the cabriole knee is vigorous but in low relief ("stringy," say some) with acanthus leaves and other foliate motifs. *Tilt-top tea tables* usually have "piecrust"—or alternating S- and C-scroll molding—on the top edge. Their pedestals are formed of a characteristic base-shaped baluster and a fluted pillar or column. Knees of New York tea tables are carved in a typically shallow manner. Mahogany and cherry are common primary woods in New York, while sweet gum and tulipwood are used in construction.

The Massachusetts Bay area

Though Boston was a mercantile center like New York, its close ties to England lent a restrained grace to its interpretation of Chippendale design. Many furniture craftsmen worked in the bay towns of Boston, Newburyport, Salem, and Roxbury. Some families—like the Frothinghams of Charlestown—produced four generations of cabinetmakers. These closed systems of family apprenticeship may have encouraged a relative conservatism in Boston furniture. Commerce was on the wane in Boston after 1740; "pinched" merchants, unwilling to pay for costly decorative options, may have preferred their furniture characteristic-

ally plain. A unique Boston form, inspired by European prototypes but made nowhere else in the Colonies during the Chippendale period, was the *bombé chest*. Named for the French verb *bomber* ("to jut out") the bombé chest often had both front and sides molded into curvilinear forms: the front was serpentine; the sides, kettle-shaped. *Blockfront furniture*, distinguished by alternately convex and concave sections on the fronts of desks and chests, was also made in the Boston area. Unlike their Newport counterparts, Boston blockfronts are relatively shallow. On two-part case pieces (for example, a desk-bookcase) blocking is confined to the base (desk) section, while the upper (bookcase) section is flat. Most Boston blockfront furniture has sturdy bracket feet, and an apron ornamented by a simple center drop. Oversize dovetail joints are a hallmark of Boston blockfront construction.

Chairs in Boston are distinguished by extremely delicate cabriole legs and slender ankles. To reinforce the apparent fragility of the Boston cabriole leg, block-and-spindle stretchers are frequently used. Chair corners are commonly blocked on the inside with rectangles of maple or pine; and the decorative carving of the knees is restrained. Chairs often have ball-and-claw feet, marked by the extreme backward curvature of the rear talons, which angle sharply away from the front. Like those of New York, Boston *easy chairs* have cone-shaped, vertical arm supports.

High chests and other case pieces typically are roofed over from back to front with a broken-arch pediment, or "bonnet top," flanked by corkscrew-shaped finials topping an urn. Pilasters (flat columns) often frame the doors of Boston *desk-bookcases*, and carving is limited to a single shell on the center drawer of upper and lower sections. Thinly cut pieces of mahogany line the drawers of much Boston furniture. White pine and red cedar are important secondary woods.

Among the better-known Boston-area cabinetmakers are Benjamin Frothingham II (1734–1809), John Cogswell (active around 1760), who produced high-quality bombé furniture, and George Bright.

Newport Chippendale

Extending into the Chippendale period, Newport's cabinetmaking tradition revolved around the Goddard and Townsend families. These unique, Quaker, furniture-making families intermarried, producing 20 craftsmen in three generations. From the 1750s to the decline of Newport's commercial prosperity after the American Revolution, Goddard-Townsend craftsmen made elegantly restrained Chippendale furniture for Newport's merchant families. Among the most distinguished members of the Goddard-Townsend group were Job Townsend (1699–1765) and his son-in-law, John Goddard (1723–1785), who was perhaps the foremost exponent of the Newport Chippendale style.

Though it was also made in Boston, *blockfront furniture* evolved first in Newport, and reached a stylistic apex there. Unlike most forms of this period, the blockfront had no English precedent, deriving instead from fanciful baroque designs of Italy and northern Europe. Newport craftsmen extended their blockfronts the entire length of

Above: Mahogany and tulipwood blockfront chest of drawers by John Townsend of Newport, Rhode Island, 1765. The Metropolitan Museum of Art, Rogers Fund, 1927. Below: Massachusetts chest of drawers, ca 1760-1789, maple and pine. Wintherthur Museum. Boston area blockfronts are much shallower than their Newport counterparts, with simple sturdy bracket feet.

double case pieces, using extremely thick slabs of mahogany to achieve unsurpassed depth. Extra wood was used to strengthen the interior surfaces of the concave sections. Newport case furniture has distinctive ogee (or S-curved) bracket feet, enclosing the decorative snail-like spiral element that is a Newport "signature."

The claw-and-ball foot—as found on Newport chairs, dressing tables, and other pieces—is somewhat elongated. There is no web between the talons, which are sometimes undercut (separated from the ball). Rear chair feet, which generally do not match the front feet, are often carved in a pad shape. Some Newport chairs, Pembroke tables, and other straight-legged pieces follow the Chinese taste, having stretchers of pierced fretwork. (John Goddard, it is said, had a copy of the *Director*.) Most Newport furniture is made of Santo Domingo or Cuban mahogany with pine as a secondary wood, and tulip poplar lining the drawers. Red cedar and maple pieces are also known.

Connecticut

In Connecticut, Chippendale furniture (often primitive or "country" in design) bears the impress of both the Philadelphia and Newport schools. Emigrant cabinetmakers like Eliphalet Chapin (1740–1807) of East Windsor brought the Philadelphia influence: Chapin's chairs have rails mortised through to the back. Connecticut *high chests* often have latticed or scrolled pediments, carved with characteristic sunburst or pinwheel motifs. The feet are ogee-bracketed, as in Newport, but connected by a distinctive gadrooned molding. Cherry, an abundant native wood, is often used in the construction of Connecticut furniture. Drawer linings are usually thickly cut of white pine.

Southern furniture

Although comparatively little is known about southern Chippendale furniture, in recent years scholars have amassed enough information to shed light on some regional characteristics. Furniture of the Chesapeake Bay area, for example, is thought to show Philadelphia taste. *Maryland side chairs* are distinguished by comparatively wide pierced splats, extending across much of the space between the vertical stiles, and by their broad ears. Ogee-molded Marlborough legs are found on many Maryland chairs. Construction is in the Philadelphia manner, with rails tenoned through the back stiles. Chair seats are braced with corner blocks of quarter-round yellow pine.

North Carolina furniture, rustic in feeling, is usually made of native walnut. It shows the stylistic influences of Pennsylvania Moravian peoples who were emigrating south and west.

Charleston, South Carolina, was a major southern center of furniture production in the Chippendale period. This gracious city of tradesmen maintained close ties to English culture. Although much furniture was imported from New England and abroad, 250 cabinetmakers worked in Charleston between 1700 and 1825. The account books of one Thomas Elfe have survived, showing that between 1768 and 1775 his shop alone turned out 1,500 pieces of furniture. Charleston furniture may have been more closely related to the illustrations in Chippendale's *Director* than to the furniture of the other Colonies. Charleston-area craftsmen made rare, four-part *breakfront bookcases*, fretted like their English prototypes. English-type *clothes presses* and *chests-on-chests* were also common. (Surprisingly, the elegant and sophisticated Charlestonians did not favor blockfront furniture or examples of bombé during the Chippendale period.)

Attributions of furniture to Thomas Elfe or unknown Charleston makers have been made partly on the basis of secondary woods. Cypress, native to Charleston, is often used to brace drawers, while red cedar is used for drawer linings (and occasionally for entire pieces of furniture). Lavish use of mahogany is also a Charleston trait: serpentine dressing chests have solid mahogany drawer fronts, and inner chair corners are often blocked with this richly grained wood. ∎

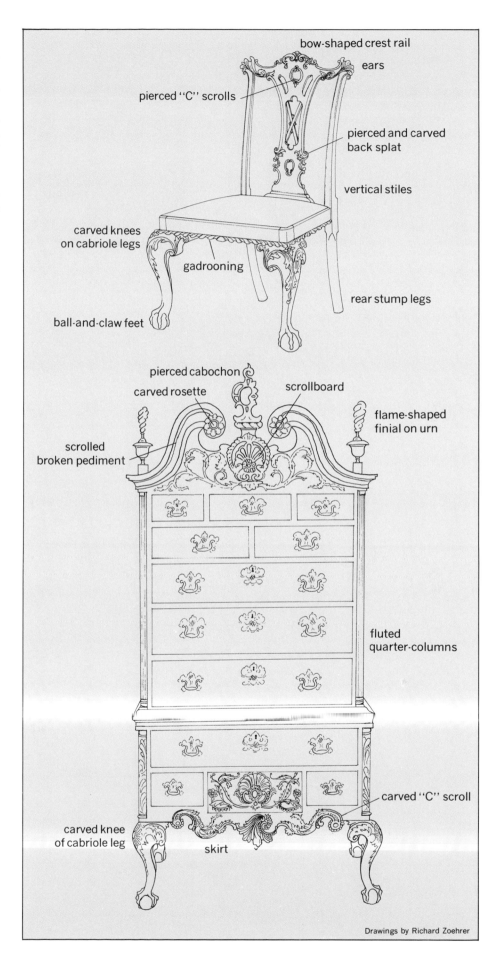

Country Chippendale

O utside the main urban centers of early America, craftsmen interpreted the Chippendale mode to satisfy their customers' wishes for moderately up-to-date furniture at the right price.

BY MARVIN D. SCHWARTZ

Country Chippendale is a style that delights people today because it is re-strained but full of surprises. The immediate point of departure for the designs is the elaborate work of urban American centers of fine furniture production and, at a remove, the fine furniture produced in England. On both sides of the Atlantic, designs derived, in large part, from Thomas Chippendale's book, *The Gentleman & Cabinet-maker's Director*. Furniture based on the engravings in this book was much more devoted to the concepts of deco-

Craftsmen outside the major Eastern cities did not lack for a sophisticated approach to furniture design, as evidenced by the astragal muntins, elaborate bonnet, and delicate carving in the desk and bookcase, opposite, made by John Shearer of Martinsburg, West Virginia. Of walnut and cherry, the desk was finished in 1801 and the bookcase added in 1806. This page: Chest of drawers, walnut, 1780–1800, believed to have been made in Alamance County, North Carolina. Note the decorative dovetailing on the bracket feet. Both pieces, Museum of Early Southern Decorative Arts, Old Salem, North Carolina.

ration than it was to practicality and function. To execute richly embellished designs like those found in the *Director*, cabinetmaker and carver joined aesthetic forces, often disregarding simple solutions and embracing complex construction.

The country interpretation was quite different. Ingenuity was substituted for elaboration; embellishments were trimmed down to preserve the spirit of the Rococo while using a minimum of parts and a minimal amount of decoration. Complex ornaments were applied in speedy ways; carving was either simplified or omitted. For instance, on the rural versions, the sleek shells of the urban chest were translated as pinwheels or fans; pierced, foliate fretwork was made into simpler lattice patterns. Flames on finials in the city version became corkscrews in the country variation.

While we know it was not necessary to be a "country" cabinetmaker to make what is known as country Chippendale, it is clear that the majority of these craftsmen were in rural settings. Their simplified designs were not altogether a result of less sophisticated skills but a response to the more modest demands of their clientele. Some rural cabinetmakers were indeed no more professional than any do-it-yourselfer. However, many were trained and had even received this training at an urban furniture-making shop. But in farming communities the demands of the patrons meant that furniture had to be economical both in construction technique and in the use of materials.

The urban cabinetmaker used imported mahogany; in the country, local woods were used—cherry, maple, and walnut, in the main. Avoiding the frills of the most lavish Chippendale designs, country craftsmen used fewer dovetails, more joinings made with mortise and tenon. Country Chippendale had straighter legs than the curving cabriole legs of its city cousins, legs that required more wood and a lot more work.

(It should be noted, however, that straight legs were also used on some high-style city-made pieces.)

The Chippendale style was fashionable in the cities in the 1760s and 1770s. As a "filtered-down" provincial expression, country Chippendale furniture naturally tends to be later, but there are examples of contemporaneous city/country productions. From what has survived and been identified, a good deal of the furniture produced in Williamsburg, Virginia, a colonial capital somewhat of a backwater, was made in the high-style period between 1760 and 1770. However, it is considered to be country Chippendale. Also, a key piece of country furniture from Connecticut is a signed desk by Benjamin Burnham that is dated 1769.

Country designs were very much subject to regional influence; much Southern furniture, Pennsylvania furniture, and furniture from various parts of New England are easily distinguishable. Furniture made in the South is the least researched of the genre, although work by scholars has recently unearthed a mine of information, and the staff of the Museum of Early Southern Decorative Arts is still working on this area's crafts. But it is known already that, aside from the urban masters in Charleston, craftsmen in the Carolinas produced a stripped-down, but fascinating, form of Chippendale.

Plain chairs with pierced splats cut out in very simple patterns, tables with plain straight legs braced with fretwork brackets, and other forms suggest Chippendale with a minimum of detail.

One outstanding form in Southern furniture is the cellarette. While the word cellarette was used on English lists of furniture before 1700, the form itself seems to have been used only rarely before 1750 and the best-known examples are Federal (1790–1815). Southern cellarettes are often in earlier styles—Queen Anne and Chippendale—but in spite of this they were probably made later. It is known that every example with some datable detail, such as a brass drawer pull, was made after the Revolution.

Along with design, it is the woods used that have aided students attempting to identify where a piece was made. In the South, walnut and cherry were popular as primary woods, as they were all over the country, but here the secondary woods used for drawer sides and braces are often yellow pine or cypress. In Pennsylvania and New York, secondary wood frequently was white pine; in New England, it was ash or oak.

Also, particular areas are known to have made idiosyncratic combinations; in Virginia there are secretaries with pedimented tops and bracketed feet that are Chippendale-derived, but they have been combined with arched doors that are a few decades earlier in feeling. German craftsmen in Virginia and the Carolinas combined traditional German elements with stylish Chippendale design.

Pennsylvania furniture reflects the diverse strains of its settlers; religious differences among the groups affected design. Quakers, as well as many German sects, demanded simplicity. In the German work there are classical pediments and curving bracket feet that show that these pieces were not uninfluenced by the elegance and flamboyance of the Philadelphia cabinetmakers, yet they still maintain their own identity. In Lancaster, a number of elaborately made pieces seem almost urban, but curiously stiff, flat carving differentiates these pieces from their stylish city counterparts.

At one time, the carved furniture of the Pennsylvania countryside was attributed to Jacob Bachman; now, thanks primarily to the research of a _____ _____ _____ John _____ der, the attributions have been re-

Opposite Page: Cherry desk and bookcase, thought to have been made about 1800 by Peter Eddleman, a cabinetmaker of the North Carolina Piedmont. The delicate string inlay on the drawers, a decorative device typical of southern Piedmont furniture, is an accomplished piece of work. Museum of Early Southern Decorative Arts. This page: Secretary-bookcase of pine and maple, made in Massachusetts ca 1765. Decorative grain of the door panels, carved pinwheels, and sprightly bracket feet on this well-proportioned piece bespeak its anonymous maker's sense of good design. Bernard and S. Dean Levy, Inc., New York.

studied. It may be a while before definitive statements can be made, but no matter who made this Pennsylvania country Chippendale furniture, it is distinctive and reflects a strong taste. Rococo ornament has been regularized, flattened, and executed in a way that makes it reminiscent of Continental peasant ornamentation.

Upstate New York furniture, products made in the vicinity of Albany, and New Jersey examples seem to relate to one another. Perhaps it was the combination of Dutch and English backgrounds in both places that created similar tastes. The fact that the use of the large wardrobe, or *kas*, was common to these areas, and that this seventeenth century form continued to be built well into the nineteenth century, suggests that the Dutch heritage was particularly influential.

Both in upstate New York and in New Jersey, Chippendale gentlemen's presses (pieces with doors over a set of drawers and topped by a prominent cornice) were also popular, possibly because they were updated versions of the *kas*. Also in favor were chairs with yoke-shaped backs and Chippendale pierced splats, combined with rush seats and legs turned in a William and Mary style. (However, that odd combination popped up all over New England as well.)

Connecticut cabinetmakers were among the most ingenious of the country Chippendale designers. Connecticut towns were often large enough to support a good cabinetmaker, though not affluent enough for the output to be as lavishly executed as work in the major centers of fashion. In many cases the ornament is extensive, but almost always translated into motifs that are less time-consuming to make than those encountered on work from Newport or Philadelphia.

Leaves may become scales or fluting. Shells, rosettes, and the whole repertory of classical ornament that played an important role in urban designs were modified—but with skill. It is not that the carvers were amateurs, it is simply that they were producing for their own customers and did not have practice in more elaborate work. On examples with claw and ball feet, it is interesting to see how well the feet are carved most of the time. Benjamin Burnham's 1769 desk rests on well-carved claw and ball feet, yet the leaf carving on the knees just above is obvious country work, deep but more stylized than on urban examples. Connecticut chests with shells over blockfronts are almost as urban as anything made in Newport, but each has a detail or two rendered with a certain stiffness that connoisseurs today regard as naive charm.

Since the story that the gifted Newport cabinetmaker John Townsend spent some time in Connecticut as a refugee from the Revolutionary War fighting in Newport has proved apocryphal, the source for the provincial interpretations of his kind of design is mysterious. Whatever their origin, the blockfront chests of Connecticut origin are special.

More typical of work in that state are post-Revolutionary examples in which Chippendale designs are simplified to conform to country taste. On chest-on-chests, the pediments have stylized pierced work; shell ornaments on chairs and chests are reduced to almost abstract designs. On some very simple pieces only the curve of a bracketed foot or the molding along a skirt belie their relationship to Chippendale.

A number of cabinetmakers who worked in Connecticut have been identified and quite a few extant pieces can be attributed to them, but it will take more research to be sure of exactly who made what. For example, Aaron Roberts had been thought to be the chief cabinetmaker, but we now know that few of the pieces attributed to him are his work. There is a chest signed by Bates How in the Garvan collection at Yale, yet little is known about what else he made.

The elaborately inlaid designs on the slant-front walnut desk on the opposite page, made in Chester County or Lancaster County, Pennsylvania in 1771, recall the spirited Germanic influence of the region's
painted dower chests. Brasses on this piece are original, and the name
"Reese" is branded on the slanted front panel below the inlaid date. Private collection, photo courtesy Israel Sack, Inc. This page: Connecticut desk, made in 1769 and bearing the signature of Benjamin Burnham. The sophisticated blockfront treatment of this desk invites
comparison to the consummate formal furniture of Newport, but its idiosyncratic apron design and solid cherry construction belie its country
origins. The Metropolitan Museum of Art.

The gentleman's press above, made in New Jersey between 1760 and 1780, does not have its original brasses. Constructed of cherry, its fine proportions suggest its maker's familiarity with the high-style furniture of nearby Philadelphia. Yet its sturdy simplicity is in the best tradition of rural New Jersey and Pennsylvania, where Quaker values held sway. Note the finely shaped bracket feet, fluted pilasters, recessed door panels, and neatly molded cornice. The New Jersey Historical Society, gift of the estate of Frederick I. Canfield.

The Garvan chest is a tantalizing piece in that it has the same simplified gadrooning as the 1801 chest signed by Reuben Beman, Jr. of Kent, Connecticut, but it has very clumsily shaped claw and ball feet.

In New Hampshire, a broad range of cabinetwork was executed. Some of the outstanding pieces are urban in spirit, generally assumed to have been made in Portsmouth, but there are many examples that reflect the rural taste. As with Connecticut country furniture, the Rococo ornament was modified or stylized, and local woods were favored over imported. The best group of rural furniture has been attributed to one family, the Dunlaps, who operated out of several small New Hampshire towns. Their case pieces have elaborate moldings in flowered ogee patterns, distinctive shells, and additional, busy decorative details. Dunlap chairs are made in the tall, thin proportions of the William and Mary style, but the details—straight legs, yoke-shaped top rails, and pierced splats—are Chippendale. Town or country in origin, their basic straight-line construction, combined with busy carved motifs, make New Hampshire furniture readily identifiable.

Wherever its colonial origin, there is an overall consistency to the country approach that imbues all of it with a very decided charm. It does not require the knowledge that a corkscrew finial is a frankly economical way of interpreting the flame motif in order to find it engaging. In the same way, rope-twists in place of the more elegant fluting on columns are fun to behold. Country Chippendale cabinetmakers, as a group, tempered and translated elaborate Rococo ornament to satisfy a clientele that wanted moderately up-to-date designs—at the right price. These demands produced a distinctly American kind of furniture. ∎

The Dunlap family, employing as many as 52 workers, dominated cabinetmaking in late 18th century New Hampshire. Major John Dunlap, working in Bedford, New Hampshire, made the high chest of drawers at left for Jane Walker in 1782, according to records in his account book. Of maple and pine, the chest illustrates John Dunlap's technique of using eye-catching ornament on both the top and bottom of a piece. Note the similarity of this piece's prominent "ears" and its shell carving to those details on the chair above, made by Samuel or John Dunlap I or II in Salisbury. The chair is constructed of local maple with a floral needlework seat cover. The Metropolitan Museum of Art.

Connecticut Blockfront Design

As the blockfront style spread from Boston through the towns of 18th-century New England, specific regions developed their own local variants.

BY MINOR MYERS, JR.

Like regional speech patterns, American furniture of the mid-18th century shows strong local variations. Because basic styles varied slightly from town to town, you can chart the evolution of design across the New England landscape as individual towns—particularly in New London County, Connecticut—developed their own variants of shapes and ornaments.

It is hard to find a better example of the movement of a style through the colonies than that of blockfront-design development as it progressed from Bos-

ton in the 1730s, to Newport in the 1750s and 1760s, to New London County in the late 1760s and 1770s, and to the upper Connecticut River valley at the end of the 18th century.

The specific steps by which designs moved from one town to another are difficult to document. But merchants, craftsmen, and travelers all played a role in the process. Craftsmen might apprentice in one town, then move to a distant area, carrying their master's style with them. Merchants and traders regularly shipped furniture as part of their cargoes. For example, in 1773 the New London, Connecticut, merchant Nathaniel Shaw received a desk ordered from John Goddard of Newport. Before he resold it to a Hartford merchant, it is quite likely that one of the cabinetmakers who worked regularly for Shaw had a chance to study this

Newport desk for inspiration while it was still in New London. Travelers might well ask for styles they had seen in neighboring or distant towns, and their confused recollections of an impressive piece thus account for the hybrid variations of styles in "made-to-order" pieces.

Tracking a style across the map requires careful attention to details of ornament and construction, for often only a subtle characteristic of decoration or form marks the work of a particular town or cabinetmaker. Pieces with inscriptions or good family provenance are thus extraordinarily valuable to the student trying to attribute specific stylistic variations to a particular place and time. Such documented pieces are the anchors with which tentative attributions may be secured.

The blockfront style, often consid-

ered one of America's great contributions to furniture design, is documented in Boston as early as 1738, the year Job Coit and Job Coit, Jr., signed a secretary now at the Winterthur Museum. The style takes its name from the raised panels or "blocking" applied to either side of the drawer fronts. Blockfront furniture also has a recessed center panel between the two raised surfaces. As in many later Massachusetts pieces, the blocking in the Coit desk is rounded rather simply at the top.

In eastern Massachusetts, as elsewhere, the blockfront was readily adaptable to large case pieces. Always limited to fairly costly furniture, it became a fashionable way to design desks, secretaries, chests, and double chests in the Queen Anne and Chippendale modes popular through much of the 18th century. There are a few blockfront lowboys, but only rarely was the blockfront applied to highboys.

Blockfront design in Massachusetts

The typical Massachusetts four–drawer chest of the late 18th century had claw-and-ball feet with the blocking carried straight up the surface of each drawer with no rounding on the top drawer. Such rounding or squaring, however, appeared on Massachusetts desks and secretaries. Some Massachusetts cabi-

This page: Chest-on-chest by an unidentified Norwich, Connecticut cabinetmaker, 1775-1800. Late Norwich blockfront design features full blocking in the base with shallow or no blocking in the top section. Other Norwich details: heavily scalloped skirt, rich carving, short ball-and-claw feet. Opposite page: detail of Newport-like shells carved with alternately concave and convex rays. Both photographs courtesy Israel Sack Inc., New York.

Above: secretary-bookcase signed by Job Coit, Sr. of Boston and dated 1738. Black walnut and pine. Although this is the earliest documented example of Boston blockfront design, the blocking is rounded rather simply at the top as in many later Boston pieces. The Henry Francis duPont Winterthur Museum. Opposite, top: On this typical late 18th-century eastern Massachusetts blockfront chest, the blocking is carried straight up the front, with no rounded arch on the top drawer. Note typical heavy front ball-and-claw feet and rather unusual rear bracket feet. Opposite, bottom: Some eastern Massachusetts cabinetmakers—like the unidentified designer of this kneehole desk—gave the blocking a rounded contour quite distinct from the sharper squared blocking of Rhode Island or Connecticut. Both courtesy Historic Deerfield; photos Helga Studio.

netmakers gave the blocking a rounded countour (almost like a serpentine surface) rather than the sharper, squared effect popular in Rhode Island and Connecticut. The bureau table or kneehole desk, an impressive blockfront form, was also made in Massachusetts. In this state (as somewhat later in Norwich, Connecticut), a chest-on-chest might have a blockfront base with a plain-fronted top.

Newport: the Goddard-Townsend shells

In 1756 the blockfront became fashionable in Newport, where it received new treatment at the hands of John Townsend. In that year Townsend, a consummate craftsman, produced a small document chest with the blocking surmounted by carved scallop shells. This little chest with its inscription is the first accurately dated example of the block-and-shell treatment that the Townsend and Goddard cabinetmaking families of Newport developed to perfection during the next three decades. Their work was expensive, and the most fully articulated examples of the style were surely limited to houses of considerable wealth. In the 1760s John Townsend created chests with shells carved at the top of the blocking. He also crafted desks with the shells on the fall (the hinged front panel that concealed the writing surface and storage nooks) as a continuation of the blocking on the drawers below. Another costly but elegant variation was the kneehole desk or bureau table in which the basic Massachusetts form was treated with more vigorous blocking decorated by shells. Probably the ultimate development of the style was the nine-shell secretary with a full set of carvings on the drawers, the front fall, and the bookcase doors.

In Providence, cabinetmakers soon adopted the block-and-shell style. Although their work often resembles that of the Newport makers, many Providence pieces are distinguished by somewhat heavier design and near-architectural decoration.

Blockfront variations in New London County, Connecticut

By the late 1760s the style had migrated to eastern Connecticut. In 1769 Isaac Fitch of Lebanon in New London County produced a blockfront desk, now at Yale University Art Gallery, for Jonathan Trumbull, who later became the second Connecticut governor to bear that name. Trumbull's desk had simple blocking without shells, but unlike the earlier Coits, Fitch more or less squared off the blocking rather than leaving it rounded on the top drawer. In that same year, 1769, Benjamin Burnham of nearby Colchester also produced a blockfront desk without shells. It too had rather squared blocking.

Sometime between 1769 and 1773, Burnham produced a three–drawer blockfront chest adorned with shells. The simple rays of his shells were a far cry from the sophisticated carvings of Newport's Goddard-Townsend clan, yet they showed a country cabinetmaker's best attempt to reproduce the high-style models of Rhode Island's cosmopolitan shipping center. But New London County cabinetmakers, particularly in the towns of Colchester and Norwich, were quick to improve their techniques. Later block-and-shell work has the Newport pattern of alternating convex and concave rays in the shells, although the Connecticut workers never quite achieved the subtleties of the consummate Rhode Island carvers. Connecticut shells have fewer and less sinuous rays, and the center fan in each shell is invariably simpler.

Between 1769 and 1788, another prominent Colchester cabinetmaker, Samuel Loomis, produced a tour-de-force version of the Connecticut block-front style in a chest-on-chest now at the Wadsworth Atheneum in Hartford. In that piece the blocking begins in the skirt and continues up over the drawers of both sections, terminating in the distinctive shells that became characteristic of Loomis and of Colchester work in general. As in the Burnham chest, there are no concave rays in the shells carved on each side. The shell in the center, however, consists primarily of concave rays; unlike the Newport prototype, it does not match the shells at the sides. The Loomis chest-on-chest also has butterfly tails on the shells, a detail that appears on a number of Colchester pieces. The exuberant carving of Loomis's shells is complemented by rope-twist columns, intricately turned twist finials, a double-dentil molding, and carved plinth (the decoration between the two cutouts in the bonnet). There are at least two other chests of very similar design.

Ornaments from such blockfront work could also be applied to other forms, where there is no blocking at all. One eastern Connecticut bonnet-top highboy has a fan in the top clearly adapted from the center shell of the blockfront design, and a New London County chest-on-chest has a block-front-type shell carved in low relief.

In the last quarter of the 18th century, workers in Colchester and Norwich produced a number of block-and-shell chests that are notable for their short ball-and-claw feet, a device the Newport cabinetmakers did not favor for such chests. Massachusetts cabinetmakers used heavier ball-and-claw feet, but their work is distinguished from that of eastern Connecticut because it lacked the shells at the sides. Another group of New London County

three–drawer block-and-shell chests cannot yet be attributed to one town; all examples of this distinctive group have a heavy ogee foot edged with a raised beading.

In Norwich, cabinetmakers developed their own version of the blockfront chest-on-chest, far different and more restrained than the characteristic Colchester designs. Norwich work typically had blocking, with or without shells, in the base with very light blocking or a plain surface in the top. (This was also a typical Massachusetts arrangement.) Like their Colchester neighbors, Norwich cabinetmakers had a propensity for intricate ornament. They added rich carving and heavily scalloped skirts to case furniture.

Nearby Preston also followed Rhode Island's lead, but in somewhat different ways. While no blockfront chests from the town have been identified, several clock cases with shells inspired by the Rhode Island blockfronts do survive. The most notable example is the Thomas Harland clock, now in the Detroit Institute of Arts, which has the name of a Preston cabinetmaker, Abishai Woodward, inscribed on its face. A finely carved shell surmounts a raised panel or blocking, in just the same manner as the Rhode Island clocks.

Although neighboring Lisbon produced no identified pieces in the block-and-shell style, it too was under Rhode Island influence. A chest-on-chest now at the Connecticut Historical Society could well be mistaken for Rhode Island work, were it not inscribed "Lisbon 1796." In typical Townsend-Goddard fashion, it has a simple bonnet decorated with raised panels of the sort that were quite frequently used on

Left: Secretary-bookcase made by the Goddard-Townsend family of Newport, Rhode Island between 1760 and 1785. Originally made for Joseph Brown of Providence, this nine-shell secretary is a superb example of Goddard-Townsend blockfront design, with a full set of shell carvings on the drawers, front fall, and bookcase doors. Note typical Newport bonnet treatment, with simple raised panels. Furniture made by the Goddard-Townsend clan was expensive and the most fully articulated examples of the style were limited to houses of considerable wealth. Rhode Island Historical Society, Providence.

Newport blockfront secretaries.

The town of New London was the tenth largest American city in the 1770s when it produced furniture in the Newport idiom. At the Shaw Mansion, headquarters of the New London County Historical Society, is a secretary made by Samuel Edgecomb of New London in the 1770s. It has no blocking, but like the Lisbon, Connecticut, chest, the bonnet is decorated with raised panels. Other pieces with a long New London history look so much like Newport work that they have long been considered such. But it is likely that a good many of them were produced in New London.

Despite heavy Newport influence, New London County furniture—with its many local variations—began to develop a look of its own. Where the Townsends and Goddards were restrained in their use of ornament, New London cabinetmakers embellished their furniture with an abundance of dentil moldings, rope-twist columns, gadrooned edges, highly carved plinths, and richly carved Catherine wheels (round sunburstlike ornaments often found on bonnet tops). This New London County synthesis, in turn, was influential in shaping the style that emerged in the towns along the Connecticut River.

Blockfront in the Connecticut River valley

One of the most curious variations of the blockfront style has a long history in Lyme, a town in New London County at the mouth of the Connecticut River. It is likely that both cabinetmaker and customer, familiar with the blockfront style and the newer ser-

Top right: Blockfront chest attributed to Benjamin Burnham of Colchester, Connecticut, ca 1769-1793. By the late 1760s blockfront design had emigrated from Newport to New London County. Country cabinetmakers tried to emulate sophisticated carvings of Newport's Goddard-Townsend clan. The rays of Burnham's shells, though graceful, are simpler than those of Newport. Right: Middletown produced shallowly blocked chests such as this one (ca 1780-1810) with characteristic vestigial shells and simple gadrooning at the skirt. Both photos The Webb-Deane-Stevens Museum, Wethersfield, Connecticut.

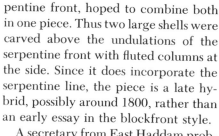

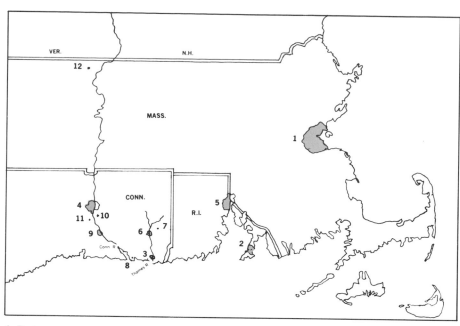

1. Boston
2. Newport
3. New London
4. Hartford

5. Providence
6. Norwich
7. Preston City
8. Old Lyme

9. Middletown
10. Glastonbury
11. Whethersfield
12. Bernardston

pentine front, hoped to combine both in one piece. Thus two large shells were carved above the undulations of the serpentine front with fluted columns at the side. Since it does incorporate the serpentine line, the piece is a late hybrid, possibly around 1800, rather than an early essay in the blockfront style.

A secretary from East Haddam probably would have been called Colchester were it not inscribed "Calvin Willey," a name which can be tied to East Haddam. It has the bonnet typical of Colchester together with simple blockfront drawers.

The Middletown area produced its own version of the block-and-shell style. Middletown blockfront chests, for example, had the same raised panels found in Rhode Island and New London County, but the shells appear only vestigially. Simple gadrooning ornaments the top edges of the rounded blocking, a far cry from the full carving produced just miles south. A late-century chest from Middletown, now owned by the Connecticut Society of Colonial Dames, is a typical example.

Glastonbury and Wethersfield cabinetmakers produced a number of highboys with ornament very similar to that found on New London County blockfront pieces, but with a distinct, and usually heavier, touch. However, no furniture designed with actual blockfronts can be attributed to these shops, even though the ornamental debt to New London County blockfront work is evident. Hartford, on the other hand, produced a variant of the blockfront design almost as removed from New London County as it was from Newport. A 1785–1810 desk, now in the Yale University Art Gallery, has incuse

Above left: Map shows progression of blockfront design from Boston area in mid-18th century through Newport in the 1750s and 1760s, New London County in the 1760s and 1770s, and the upper Connecticut River Valley by century's end. Drawing Richard Zoehrer. Left: Desk made in the Hartford area late in the 18th century has incuse rather than raised panels of blocking. Hartford blockfront design, in its relative simplicity, was as removed from the manner of New London County as it was from sophisticated Newport. Yale University Art Gallery.

rather than raised panels at the sides. Whorls resembling the top of a column, rather than a Newport shell, decorate the top drawer, while the arches carry the blocking up on to the fall.

Historic Deerfield has a blockfront chest-on-chest dating from 1780 to 1810 that brings the story full circle. It was found in Bernardstown, Massachusetts, a town less than ten miles from the Vermont border, and presumably it was made in that area. In almost every detail it copies Norwich (New London County) designs, which in turn were heavily influenced by the designs of Rhode Island and eastern Massachusetts. The base is blocked, yet the top has a plain surface decorated with columns at the sides topped by Corinthian capitals. Like the Norwich piece upon which it presumably was modeled, the Bernardstown chest-on-chest has claw-and-ball feet, but it lacks the shells on the blocked base and the scalloped skirt.

By the time the Bernardstown chest-on-chest was made—late in the 18th or very early in the 19th century—blockfront work, and the whole Chippendale style of which it was a part, began to fade from fashion in urban cabinetmaking centers. In the country, however, large Chippendale pieces remained popular as late as 1805.

Thus the blockfront generally was passé by the opening of the 19th century. Its 70-year history witnessed the creation of many great works of the American cabinetmaker's art. And its many subtle variations permit the modern student to track the fascinating evolution of this design element as it passed through the towns of 18th-century New England. ■

Right: Chest-on-chest made between 1780 and 1810. This impressive piece was found in the Bernardstown area of northwestern Massachusetts, less than ten miles from the Vermont border, bringing the geographic progression of blockfront design nearly full circle. In nearly every detail this chest emulates Norwich design: claw-and-ball feet, blocking limited to the base. But it is simpler, lacking shells on the blocking and having only a pendant shell rather than a fully carved skirt. Courtesy Historic Deerfield; photo Helga Studio.

The Kast and the Schrank

New York's Netherlands Dutch settlers and Pennsylvania's Palatinate Germans applied old world design tradition to these massive American wardrobe forms.

BY JOSEPH T. BUTLER

Wardrobes have been built over many centuries. They can be freestanding and movable, or they may be attached in some way to the interior architecture of a building. The wardrobes discussed here are all freestanding. They represent two traditions—that of the Netherlands Dutch in New York State and that of the Palatinate Germans in Pennsylvania.

The wardrobe has many national names. Those most frequently encountered in the United States are "press cupboard" for certain 17th-century New England pieces, *armoire* in areas where there is French influence, and *kast* and *schrank* in areas settled by people of Dutch or Germanic origin. Clothing and other textiles intended for domestic use were stored in such pieces.

Some extant early wardrobes date back to the beginning of the 13th century. Only a few such pieces exist today and they survive primarily because they were used in the sacristies of churches and cathedrals for the storage of ecclesiastical vestments. In decoration, they often reflect the architectural vocabulary of the then-pervasive gothic style, or they may be painted with religious scenes.

During the 16th century, a wardrobe form was developed that provided the main design source for later American pieces. Italian Renaissance design was encouraged and nurtured in the north of Europe through the patronage of the court of the French king Francis I, who died in 1547. Italian craftsmen were imported to decorate and embellish his palace at Fontainebleau. These decorations greatly inspired French designer Androuet Du Cerceau (ca 1520–84), who produced some of the earliest engraved plates of furniture designs. Circulated in France from the 1550s onward, Du Cerceau's designs often demonstrated great inventiveness and fantasy. In the Low Countries, Flemish designer Hans Vredeman de Vries

In the Hudson Valley, along Long Island's north shore, and in northern New Jersey the *kast* form was popular. These wardrobes were either plain, painted, like the example at left, or, like the unusual piece above, inlaid. This rare, late-17th-century example from Merrick, Long Island is made of oak and inlaid with walnut in geometric, sawtooth, and foliate motifs showing the influence of the Lowlands baroque design. Courtesy Henry Francis du Pont Winterthur Museum. The red gum, tulip, and pine *kast* at left, ca 1720, with its typical grisaille painting of fruit trophies suspended from a ribbon, is one of the finest surviving examples of painted *kasten*. Courtesy Monmouth County Historical Association, Freehold, New Jersey.

Dutch settlers and their descendants found the *kast* form so useful that it continued to be made well into the 19th century. Families of cabinetmakers such as the Egertons of New Brunswick, New Jersey, crafted and sold *kasten* for the better part of two centuries. The example above, of sweet gum, white pine, yellow pine, and walnut with applied molding, was made by Matthew Egerton—whose paper label is shown at right—about 1790. Note the bracket feet, showing the influence of 18th-century design on this essentially baroque form. Monmouth County Historical Association, Freehold, New Jersey.

The earliest examples have ball-turned or bun feet; some later pieces have claw-and-ball feet or brackets.

(1527–ca 1604) and his son Paul exerted a strong influence that extended also to England and to Scandinavia from the 1580s until the middle of the 17th century. Their engraved furniture designs incorporated grotesque masks and strapwork. Both Du Cerceau and Vredeman de Vries engraved designs for wardrobes that are the direct ancestors of the *kast* and *schrank*.

Lowlands design strongly influenced English taste in the 16th and early 17th centuries, a trend that was amplified by the ascension of William and Mary to the throne in 1689. William III, a Dutchman, brought many craftsmen from the Lowlands to produce decorative objects for his court. He introduced the continental baroque style that remained a strong element in English design throughout the first half of the 18th century.

Because continental and English design interacted from the 16th through the middle of the 18th centuries, emigrants from Germany, the Lowlands, and England shared common design influences. While the craftsmen who migrated to America in the 17th and early 18th centuries probably were not familiar with high-style furniture designs, they brought with them the Anglo-continental tradition, which was an integral part of their design vocabulary.

The European-inspired wardrobe type that became most popular in America is constructed in four tiers or sections. At the top is a cornice, either attached to the main body with pegs or nails, or simply resting on it. The central section is a rectangular box with shelves and two doors, which can be closed across the front. Some later examples had shelves on one side and an empty space on the other with pegs for hanging clothing. Under this is a low rectangular section, containing a drawer or drawers, which rests on detachable feet. Earliest feet are ball-turned or have balls flattened to form "bun" feet. Some later examples have claw-and-ball feet or brackets, both of

Much less sophisticated but no less charming is this painted late-17th-century *kast* from the Hudson Valley. It lacks the formal cornice at the top and the drawers beneath the doors typical of the *kast* form, and it is painted largely in grisaille with touches of pale color: note the ambitious decoration of fruit trophy swags on the sides and the front, as well as the two cherubs at the tops of the doors. The simple boot jack feet are an extension of the side panels. This *kast* was made in the Saugerties area of New York State. Sleepy Hollow Restorations, gift of Mrs. Mitchel Taradash.

Juxtaposed on this page are an elaborately inlaid Pennsylvania *schrank*, above, crafted of walnut and embellished with the name George Huber and the date, 1779, and a much less ornate Hudson Valley *kast* of red gum, tulip, and cherry (inset) also made during the third quarter of the 18th century. The *kast*'s ball-and-claw feet, executed in the squared-off style typical of New York, show Chippendale's influence on this essentially baroque form. Both *kasten* and *schranken* are massive forms that can be over seven feet tall: for mobility, they were constructed in sections that could be disassembled. *Schrank*: Philadelphia Museum of Art. *Kast*: Albany Institute of History and Art, gift of Mrs. Alan W. Carrick in memory of Russell M. Johnson.

The two types of *kasten* are those with painted decoration and those that are grained, ebonized, or wholly unadorned.

The classic pine *kast* above left, ca 1750, was produced during most of the 18th century. Note here the typical bun feet—a holdover from 17th-century design—that distinguish this *kast* from the otherwise identical Matthew Egerton example with bracket feet shown on the third page of this chapter. The Newark Museum, gift of Dr. and Mrs. E.F. Hird, 1961. Painted *kasten* like the one at right, above are much rarer than those without such decoration. This example is outstanding for the completeness of its still-intact decoration. Note the *trompe l'oeil* niches painted on the doors. The Metropolitan Museum of Art, Rogers Fund, 1909.

which are associated with the American Chippendale style.

Although there are some variations on the arrangement of sections discussed above, it is this general configuration which makes the *kast* and *schrank* a distinctive furniture form. It is important to remember that because of their massiveness, most wardrobes were constructed for easy disassembly and moving.

The *kast* has often been termed *kas* in works which deal with American furniture. However, as *kast* means cupboard in Dutch, it is the author's preferred spelling of the word. The form was particularly popular in the Hudson River Valley, along the north shore of Long Island and in northern New Jersey. Although *kasten* were being made in the late years of the 17th century, most surviving examples are from the

18th century. Several documented examples of Dutch furniture, including a *kast* presently at The Brooklyn Museum, were brought to America in the 17th century; they provided certain inspiration to American cabinetmakers.

Kasten are generally of two types—those with painted decoration and those that have grained or ebonized surfaces or that remain unadorned. The group of surviving examples with painted decoration is quite small. It numbers only about ten and most examples are in public collections. The decoration generally consists of trophies of fruit suspended from a ribbon and set in a *trompe l'oeil* niche. The painting was done in gray and white (grisaille) probably to attempt a simulation of the deep carving found on more sophisticated examples. The simplest example of this painted group does not

have a cornice drawer or separate feet, but cherubim have been added to the decoration on the doors.

A rare example of an early *kast* is preserved today in the Winterthur Museum. It was made in New York City, Kings County, or Queens County during the second half of the 17th century. It is rare because of its early date and because it is inlaid. Made of oak, it is inlaid with walnut arranged in geometric, zigzag, and leaf patterns, showing the direct influence of Lowlands baroque design.

The more common type of 18th-century *kast* is unadorned except for the use of moldings and fielded panels. The American craftsmen often forgot that the vertical areas on the sides and between the doors were traditionally ornamented with classical columns which architecturally supported the cornice above. In native examples the columns were generally reduced to a series of rectangular moldings.

Later design influences can generally be seen in the feet of *kasten*. A well-documented example has survived in which claw-and-ball feet have been substituted for the more ordinary ball or "bun" feet. The upper sections of this piece could not be distinguished from an earlier example. The heavy cornice, fielded panels, and fluted pilasters are all typical of baroque design. Another later introduction is the presence of urn-shaped drawer pulls in the Chippendale style. This *kast* belonged to Margaret Sanders (1764–1830) and was given to her when she was married to Kiliaen Van Rensselaer (1763–1845) in 1791. Family tradition states that the piece came from the Schenectady home of Mrs. Van Rensselaer's parents John and Deborah Glen Sanders.

One of the most extraordinary facts concerning the *kast* is that it was made over a very long period of time, from the 17th century through the entire 18th and into the 19th century. *Kasten* apparently appealed to the conservative people of Dutch ancestry who lived in the environs of New York City. The Egerton family of cabinetmakers in New Brunswick, New Jersey made *kasten* from the 18th into the 19th centuries. The two best-known members of the family are Matthew, Sr. (died 1802) and Matthew, Jr. (died 1837). The Monmouth County Historical Society owns an Egerton *kast*, which on the basis of its label can be dated to about 1790. Like the Albany example, this *kast* is baroque in form except for the presence of bracket feet which are associated with the Chippendale style.

In those areas of Pennsylvania settled by Palatinate Germans, the term *shonk* or *schrank* is most often used to denote the wardrobe form. *Shonk* is a variant in dialect of the High German *schrank* and the latter is most often used to describe such pieces. The emigration of Germans to Pennsylvania began in 1683 and continued with momentum until the period of the Revolution. They principally settled in southeastern Pennsylvania, introducing tra-ditional methods of cabinetmaking which were to be preserved for many generations.

The tradition of the Pennsylvania-German *schrank* has its origins in the wardrobes made in Germany and Switzerland in the late Middle Ages and Renaissance. The concept of dower furniture, which was expressed in Renaissance Italy through the cassone or dower chest, was assimilated into German and Swiss cabinetmaking. Chests and wardrobes were decorated with inlay and painting to commemorate the date of the marriage of a couple. In addition, symbols auspicious to the prospering of the marriage were included with the names or initials of the betrothed. Tulips, hearts, crowns, and birds are some of the most popular of these devices; their symbolism extends into antiquity.

This late medieval tradition was transplanted to Pennsylvania. Craftsmen did not paint hardwood furniture made of oak, walnut, and cherry. Instead, it was sometimes inlaid or left entirely without decoration. Softwood pine furniture, on the other hand, was painted with stylized decoration in bright polychrome colors. Like the *kast*, the *schrank* was conceived in four sections: a heavy cornice, a main body, a section with drawers, and feet. The two types differ chiefly in the treatment of the feet. In the *kast* the bulbous, turned feet are separate elements placed by themselves under the section with drawers. The *schrank* is conceived with a thick molding under the drawers and the "bun" feet become an integral part of it.

An early example of the *schrank* form is preserved today at the Chester County Historical Society. Made in the first half of the 18th century, the piece is unadorned except for the presence of fielded panels in the doors, sides, and base. It is less broad than most pieces of this form and perhaps shows some influence of English design. More typical of the true Pennsylvania-German proportions is a walnut *schrank* made by D. I. Mertz for Emanuel Herr and his wife, dated February 17, 1768. The fielded panels of the doors are inlaid with the names and date inside cartouches with geometric pinwheel designs below. The inlay is done in *wachseinlegan* (wax inlay), made of sulphur mixed with wax or putty. In the same tradition is a *schrank* at the Philadelphia Museum with more elaborate inlay on both the fielded panels and their frames. The panels contain crowns and birds above and stylized swastikas below. The frames are inlaid with pots of flowers, vines, stars, and pinwheels. Two drawers also contain line inlay and Chippendale pulls. The inlaid inscription, "Georg Huber Anno 1779" represents the person for whom the *schrank* was made. This piece, in addition, has a dentilled border under the cornice.

The painted softwood *schrank* did not receive the elaborate attention afforded the dower chest. In many instances, the body of the piece was painted a solid color and the fielded panels were picked out in a stippled effect which resembled marbelizing. This was often achieved through the successive application of several coats of paint with a crumpled cloth. As with the *kast*, the massive *schrank* was made so that it could easily be disassembled and moved.

Some final words of comparison of the two forms are in order. The *kast* and *schrank* both developed in America as regional vernacular forms and were popular in the areas settled by the two nationalities. Both took their inspiration from pieces made in the late Middle Ages and Renaissance and both were made in America throughout the 18th and into the 19th centuries. Most *kasten* known today, having little documentation, are difficult to date; whereas many *schranken* are carefully documented through the names, initials and dates that adorn them. The chief structural difference between the two types involves the way the feet are used. Painted examples of both types survive; however, inlay only rarely occurs in the *kast*. Although massive in scale, the *kast* and *schrank* are very popular among collectors today. Their architectural quality makes them the focal point of any room. ∎

Like the dower chests and the frakturs painted by the Pennsylvania settlers who came from Germany, this walnut *schrank* was decorated with symbolic tulips, hearts, crowns, and birds to commemorate the date of a marriage, insuring the couple a long and prosperous life. Made for Emanuel Herr and his wife, this piece is dated February 17, 1768 on the left door panel. Decoration on this so-called "Gleeder Schrank" is an inlaid, putty-like mixture of sulphur and wax. Henry Francis du Pont Winterthur Museum.

Georgia Piedmont Furniture

I *tinerant craftsmen and highly individualistic styles characterized the furniture of the Georgia Piedmont before 1820.*

BY HENRY D. GREEN

The Piedmont section of the South is the plateau that follows the foothills of the Appalachian Mountains from Virginia to Georgia. That portion of the Georgia Piedmont settled in the 18th century forms a rough triangle ranging from Augusta on the south to Athens on the west and Toccoa on the north with the Savannah river forming the eastern boundary of the state. This area, though it appears small on the map, is actually larger than the combined area of Massachusetts, Connecticut, and Rhode Island. By 1790 it had more than half the population of the state of Georgia. Here, in the last half of the 18th century, a regional style of furniture and architecture developed.

The first settlement in this area, Augusta, was established in 1735. Augusta was also the terminus of the Great Wagon Road, which ran west from Philadelphia and turned south at Williamsport, Maryland. It continued down the Valley of Virginia to Fincastle, Virginia, turned southeast to Salem, North Carolina and Camden, South Carolina, then turned west to Augusta. This was the route taken by nearly all the settlers of Georgia in the 18th century. The great majority of these settlers were of Scotch-Irish descent. Some came directly from Ulster in Northern Ireland. Some were second or third generation colonials who had lived in Virginia or western North Carolina.

The Piedmont developed, culturally speaking, as an area separate and dis-

Facing page: Sideboard of mahogany and southern yellow pine, ca 1790. This outstanding piece is distinguished by the deep serpentine curve of its facade and by fluted legs that end in spade feet cut from the same piece of wood. Author's collection. Left: Chest of drawers, walnut and southern yellow pine, ca 1790. Drawerfronts are cockbeaded and decorated with string inlay. Author's collection. Above: Corner cupboard of walnut and southern yellow pine, made between 1780 and 1800 in the Georgia Piedmont. Note graduated door panels, of which the top pair are cross-banded. Massive cornice has band of pierced holes above the dentils. Cut from one piece of wood, the base and skirt are supported on straight bracket feet. Courtesy Mr. and Mrs. A. Felton Jenkins, Jr.

tinct from Savannah and the coast, Savannah was tied by trade with England, Charleston, the West Indies, and the Eastern seaboard cities. The furniture and architecture there bears little relationship to that of the Piedmont.

The houses the people in the Piedmont built were much like the houses they left. Most of them were simple Georgian style with a porch across the front, large rooms on each side of a central hall with stairs rising to the second floor. Across the back was a sloping roof with three small shed rooms. These rooms usually had no chimneys. In some houses the center shed room was not enclosed and was left open to form a porch under the main roof. The kitchen was a separate building connected to the main house by a covered walkway. Chimneys rose the full height of the house at each end of the two main rooms. Sometimes the houses were a story and a half.

The main rooms had wainscoting, above which the walls were either plastered or sheathed in horizontal pine boards. The ceilings were wide pine boards like the floors. The woodwork in these rooms was painted with bright colors of blue, green, red, brown, and yellow. Often the colors contrasted. Occasionally the panels below the chair rails were lined with cut corners like the inlay on much of the furniture. At times stippling was used as decoration on the wainscoting and mantles. The mantles built up from wooden moldings were usually very high, balancing the high ceilings. The windows, doors, moldings, and fanlight show craftsmanship of the first order. Various shapes and designs of dentil molding were popular. The pilasters on the sides of the mantles were reeded or fluted,

70

and sunburst carving was used in various shapes and sizes. This same type of construction was used around the tops of desks and bookcases and corner cupboards. However, sunburst carving has yet to be found on any of the furniture. In fact, carving of any kind is extremely rare on the furniture.

Very little is known about the identity of the early cabinetmakers in the Georgia Piedmont. One cabinetmaker identified by family records was William Simpson, who was born in Virginia in 1778 and was brought to Wilkes County, Georgia that same year. He built a handsome house there in 1812 and is credited with several pieces of furniture still owned by his descendants.

Simpson's story substantiates the belief that the cabinetmakers, or joiners, also built houses. Early collectors and dealers of Georgia Piedmont furniture always reported that the cabinetmakers were itinerant. Because there were no towns in the area, with the exception of Augusta, these men travelled about the countryside in wagons and made whatever was ordered. This is what gives the Georgia furniture so much originality and charm.

The general quality of the pieces from the Augusta area would indicate that there were also skilled cabinetmakers working there. For example, the *Augusta Chronicle* in 1793 listed Jeremiah Burdine as a cabinetmaker.

However, even in Augusta, no signed or marked pieces of furniture have ever been found.

Woods of the Piedmont

The Piedmont was covered with a great variety of hard woods. The woods grown in Georgia are darker in color and have a more pronounced grain than woods grown in New England, because different growth conditions affect their texture, color, and chemical composition. The wood gets lighter and shows less grain as we move northward, a characteristic that is particularly helpful in identifying southern furniture.

In Georgia cabinetwork, the principal woods used were pine, walnut,

Opposite page: Chest of drawers, walnut and southern yellow pine, ca 1790. Drawerfronts are cockbeaded and decorated with string inlay. Feet are cut from solid side boards; front skirt is veneered. Strip molding is applied ¼″ below top, and there are blind locks on the two top drawers. Two other identically constructed chests, with different inlay, are known. Author's collection. Above: Huntboard, ca 1800, an indigenous southern form. This example, of southern yellow pine, may be unique in its use of platform-topped posts, which are joined with pegs. There is a small drawer suspended inside the cupboard compartment. Note inlaid diamond escutcheons. Courtesy Mr. & Mrs. J.H. Hilsman Collection.

birch, maple, and cherry. Mahogany was rarely used in the Piedmont because of the difficulty of transporting it from the coast. However, when mahogany was used, the furniture was usually well made and of very fine quality.

The pine grown in Georgia is a very distinctive wood. It is dense, heavy, free of knots, and can be cut in large widths, well suited for cabinetwork and for building houses. It is soft and easy to work when freshly cut, and becomes hard with age. It has a very sharp red grain that is quite easy to identify. Best known as "southern yellow pine," its botanical name is *Pinus teada*. Early Georgia cabinetmakers not only used it as a secondary wood for drawer linings and interior construction, but as primary wood in some handsome pieces.

Walnut, the most popular wood for cabinetwork, was abundant. This *Juglans nigra*, or native black walnut, has a dark rich grain and takes an excellent polish. With age, it often looks like mahogany. It also occurred in great widths: one early chest of drawers has a top 24 inches wide made of a single piece of walnut.

The next most widely used was yellow birch, *Betula lutea* or *Betula alleganiesis*. Birch when freshly cut has a rosy hue which darkens with age. It has a fine close grain, a soft, almost golden color, and takes a beautiful polish. In early days of collecting, if a piece was found having a very pretty soft golden color, but the wood was unknown, it was usually called fruitwood or applewood. Microscopic analysis of such a wood sample, however, usually shows it is yellow birch. In some cases, pieces thought to be maple turn out to be birch.

Southern red maple, *Acer rubrum*, commonly called swamp maple, is not as hard as that grown further north. It is found principally on bottom land and has a darker grain and color than the northern maple. The cherry wood used by Georgia Piedmont cabinetmakers, *Prunus serotina*, is commonly called black cherry.

These woods grew in plentiful supply in Georgia and were used not only as primary woods, but occasionally as

secondary woods as well. Yellow pine and tulip poplar, however, were the woods most widely used in interior construction, although drawer sides and table wings of white oak have also been found.

Forms of Georgia Piedmont furniture

The two most unusual forms of furniture made in the Georgia Piedmont are huntboards and cellarets. Huntboards appear to be almost exclusively Southern. They were made in large numbers in the latter part of the 18th and early 19th centuries in a wide variety of styles and with varying degrees of sophistication. The origins of both the form and name are obscure; the term huntboard does not appear in old wills or inventories, and most explanations for the name seem more fanciful than authentic.

From close inspection, the author is confident that nearly all huntboards made of pine, poplar, and birch were originally painted, although it is rare to find any with the original paint. This could be a clue to their use which may well have been on the oustide porches or around kitchens where weather and wear took their toll. Some examples have been found where the original paint was painted over in later years. When collectors acquired these pieces, that original paint left was in such deplorable condition that the remainder was taken off and the piece refinished down to the grain. Huntboards made of walnut, cherry and sometimes birch, however, were never painted; they were decorated with inlaid escutcheons, stringing, and cock beading.

One known example has a slight serpentine on the front of the case, but the top is straight and does not follow the bow in the end drawers. Such features seem to indicate that hardwood huntboards were probably intended for use in dining rooms rather than in kitchens or on porches. Huntboards differ from sideboards in that they stand tall on long legs which support short cases. Sideboards, by contrast, are shorter and have deeper cases. Their drawers always fit the frames. The point to em-

phasize is that huntboards follow no set pattern or period style. They come in a wide variety of shapes and sizes, in narrow and broad widths with a random arrangement of drawers and doors. Some have no drawers. One of their great charms is that no two identical examples have ever been found.

The cellarets also have great variations in design, but in contrast to huntboards, they are very sophisticated and stylish. The legs are usually tapered. Some have mixing slides. They usually have tops that lift to reveal an interior divided into compartments for bottles, or a single large drawer divided in the same way. Cabinetmakers used a great variety of inlays and veneers and lavished decoration on cellarets; as a result, they are delightful small pieces of furniture.

Sideboards were extremely popular and large numbers have survived. These are usually very high styled in the manner of the Federal period, with ornamental use of various inlays and veneers.

Georgia dining tables were all made with drop leaves. They are found with four legs or, in most instances, six legs. The more elaborate have table ends that can be moved into place to give additional seating space. Some, in two sections, have one extra leaf on each end that can be raised and supported by a single leg. The legs were made in many styles: straight and tapered legs with and without inlay, and turned legs that are plain, reeded, or twisted.

A large number of desks have been found, mostly of the slant-lid type. The lids are made with cleats at each end, for good solid construction. The cleats are solid pieces whose grain runs perpendicular to that of the main lid, and

at times they are mitred at the outside corners. Some desks have bookcase tops, but most do not. The bureau type desk and bookcase is very rare.

The desks and chests of drawers follow the simple forms of Chippendale and Hepplewhite. In Georgia, it is the author's belief that these styles were made simultaneously over a period of about 40 years.

The wills of the period list numerous other households furnishings: folding tables, birch tables, pine tables, walnut desks, blanket chests, beds with curtains, silver tablespoons, teaspoons, and silver serving pieces. The wills also list

all kinds of clocks, cupboards, flax wheels, spinning wheels, and looms. It is interesting to read the wide variety of chairs listed in the wills: riding chairs, table chairs, sitting chairs, easy chairs, common chairs, and Windsor chairs. Despite these numerous listings, chairs are the rarest form of early Georgia furniture to be found today. They are almost non-existent.

Windsor chairs were made in Georgia but few have been found; these are very plainly made with flat top rails and seats of poplar rather than the white pine most often used in New England. There is a record of a Wind-

sor chair maker in Milledgeville who made chairs for the state capitol building which was constructed in 1807. It is also recorded that on September 26, 1812, the Board of State Commissioners ordered the Treasury to pay to "Mr. John Furlow the sum of eighty-four dollars it being for forty-two Windsor chairs at two dollars each in addition to those heretofore made and delivered by him for use of the Senate and House of Representatives." None of these chairs have been identified.

Corner cupboards were made in large numbers and a great number still exist. They are made mostly of pine and

Georgia Piedmont furniture has a solid, honest style, good proportions, and nice moldings. Where curves are used they are sharp and distinct. Inlay is the primary decoration.

walnut, but a few are made of maple and birch. One regional characteristic is that they are all made in one piece. Usually they have a center molding across the front that gives the appearance of two pieces, but the sides and backing are always vertical boards running the full height of the cupboard. They are free standing; there is only one known example of a cupboard that is built into the house.

Decoration

Georgia Piedmont furniture is decorated primarily with inlay in a variety of motifs: simple stringing, fans, stars, vines, bellflowers, thistles, tulips, and jonquils. Simple stringing on drawer and door fronts often has a cut-corner pattern of quarter rounds; at other times the stringing at the ends curves back to cross itself, forming pointed ovals. Around the edges of the drawer fronts, both cock beading in dark and light woods and gouge carving simulating beading are used. The woods used for inlay are maple, holly, or dogwood. Barber-pole inlay—which is rarely seen in Georgia furniture—and triple-line inlay often make use of cherry as the contrasting wood.

Georgia Piedmont furniture has a solid, honest style, good proportions, and nice moldings. Where curves are used they are sharp and distinct. These characteristics, enhanced by quality woods and inlay, give it great beauty.

After the War of 1812, with trade embargos lifted, the wealth of the Southern planters increased. They had money to spend on good living. French influence in furniture styles and the new popularity of Greek Revival architecture were reflected in decoration and design of the beautiful homes that were being built all across the cotton belt of Georgia. The neoclassical, and later the Empire furniture, used in these ante-bellum houses was largely made in Northern factories and sold by merchants, marking the end of the itinerant craftsman and the highly individualistic styles that characterize the furniture of the Georgia Piedmont. ∎

Opposite page: Worktable at top, ca 1800, is constructed of walnut, maple, popular, and southern yellow pine. Mahogany-veneered drawer fronts are typically inlaid with cut-corner stringing. Below it is a black walnut and southern yellow pine chest-of-drawers, ca 1790-1800. Note deep serpentine front and chamfered corners inlaid with stringing. This page, above: Cellaret, ca 1790-1800, mahogany and southern yellow pine, inlaid with vine-and-thistle motif and cut-corner stringing on drawer front. At right, cellaret on frame, ca 1790-1800, walnut and southern yellow pine, in the form of a compartmented box. Skirt has gouged line carving; legs and feet are one piece. All, author's collection.

Virginia's Raised-Panel Forms

House joiners on Virginia's Eastern shore produced an enduring and distinctive style of furniture based on raised panel construction.

BY MARILYN S. MELCHOR

Virginia's Eastern Shore, a peninsula of land between the Chesapeake Bay and the Atlantic Ocean, retains much of the rural, agricultural atmosphere of its colonial days, with many small towns and settlements on the multitudinous creeks and inlets that cut through its flat, sandy landscape. Court records, which survive in unbroken continuity from 1622, show that in 1624 Virginia's Eastern Shore had a population of 76 settlers. Their household furnishings were limited to a few necessary pieces

are known only through mention in of furniture—perhaps a six-board chest, a bed or two, a table and some chairs— to fill domestic needs until other priorities could be attended. Survival in the New World depended on cleared fields and harvested crops. As the 17th century progressed into the 18th, and life became easier, the number and diversity of household objects increased.

As in other areas of the North American colonies, many different forms of furniture were used on the Shore. Some

wills, inventories, account books, and port records, for changing tastes relegated many items to the discard heap long before they were worn out, while such well-used items as chairs and textiles had only a brief life-span. Many early pieces were imported from England, as most Eastern Shore settlers came originally from that country or from Scotland. The planter/factor economic system favored in the southern colonies also encouraged the importation of British goods: colonial planters shipped their tobacco harvest to England in care of mercantile agents, who also functioned as purchasing agents for the planters, debiting their crop accounts for purchases made abroad.

Although colonial roads were poor, water travel was efficient, and the many creeks and inlets of the Eastern

Freestanding bookcases are not often mentioned in early Eastern Shore records, and only three extant examples are known. The walnut bookcase on the facing page, far left, ca 1750, was used by the Northampton County Clerk of Courts. Like the other two documented Eastern Shore bookcases, this one has solid board ends instead of the usual panel frame assembly. Courtesy The Association for the Preservation of Virginia Antiquities. Above: Flat-wall cupboard, ca 1820, in yellow pine, originally painted green with white trim. This form provided a freestanding substitute for the popular built-in or architectural cupboards. Lower door panel design derives from Salmon's *Palladio Londinensis*, Plate XXIII. Collection of Ms. Margaret Revell. This page, left: Corner cupboard in yellow pine, ca 1780. Note the well-executed fluted pilasters and paneled plinths, which—in common with examples of Shore architecture—were influenced by Salmon's designs. Originally the cupboard was painted green and white. Private Collection.

Shore became points of entry for British goods, which were cleared through a local customs official. This same ease of access to Eastern Shore plantations and small towns fostered an active intercoastal trade with the New England colonies, which is confirmed by early probate records as well as Naval Office Returns—official records of port traffic that detail cargo inventories. New England furniture was purchased by Eastern Shore dwellers, who also imported furniture made on the mainland of Virginia, most likely in Williamsburg or Norfolk, according to other documentary sources.

Perusal of wills and inventories reveals that household furnishings were also made on the Shore itself. Among the most interesting and distinctive pieces of locally made furniture are raised-panel case pieces created for Eastern Shore residents by the same craftsmen who built their homes. There are numerous surviving examples of this type of furniture, which displays distinctive regional characteristics. The raised-panel furniture group, which includes clothes presses, blanket chests, flat-wall cupboards, bookcases, turkey-breast cupboards, and corner cupboards, first appeared in the second quarter of the 18th century. The pieces are utilitarian, adaptable to diverse uses, heavily constructed, and rather large in size—all factors that have con-

The most unusual form of Eastern Shore furniture is the turkey-breast cupboard, so named for the sharply angular protrusion of its doors. The example at right, constructed of yellow pine ca 1790, was originally painted red overall, an unusual color for Shore raised panel pieces. Bold crown and waist moldings are typical of this form. Private Collection. Above: astral corner cupboard of yellow pine, ca 1800, is notable for its panel door design, directly inspired by Plate XXVI in Salmon's *Palladio Londinensis*. In this case, the panel is carved from a solid piece of wood, but other examples of astral panels found on Shore blanket chests are panel frame assemblies. Cupboard, courtesy Ann Woods Ltd.

tributed to their survival. While some pieces have left the Shore for various museums and private collections, most known examples are still owned by Shore families.

The raised panel, the distinctive and unifying element of this furniture group, was an architectural feature widely used by house joiners throughout colonial America in the 18th and early 19th centuries. House joiners working on the Shore produced both the house paneling and the raised-panel furniture. Numerous Eastern Shore houses, with raised paneling intact, testify to the skill of these craftsmen.

One popular, common design source, William Salmon's *Palladio Londinensis*, first published in 1734, accounts for the similarity between the architectural paneling and the furniture paneling. Salmon's house joiner's design book, which was published in nine editions before 1774, emphasizes the varied arrangements of raised panels, as well as the use of fluted pilasters and paneled plinths. Eastern Shore house joiners used these varied panel arrangements in both house interiors and on raised-panel furniture and they used Salmon's book well into the 19th century. Salmon advocated mixing rectangular, square, arched, astral, and cross panels—arranging and rearranging the different types of panels to produce a multitude of effects. Only his own imagination and skill limited the Eastern Shore house joiner in designing extremely pleasing house paneling or raised-panel furniture inspired by Salmon's example. Although raised-panel furniture was constructed in other areas of the colonies, only on the Eastern Shore of Virginia are there so many pieces exhibiting such varied panel arrangements. Several artisans occasionally collaborated on the construction of a piece of raised-panel furniture.

Yellow pine and black walnut are native Virginia woods. Black walnut, with its handsome color and grain, and yellow pine, because of its abundance, are the two main woods used in raised-panel furniture. Minor amounts of tulip poplar and white pine have also been found, seldom as the primary wood in this type of furniture, but more often as a secondary wood.

Walnut furniture needed no embellishment; its color and grain produce a most pleasing effect. Yellow pine, on the other hand, was usually painted. By the standards of today's taste, this effect might seem a bit garish: the piece of furniture almost always was painted a strong green or blue, while the beveled areas around the raised panels, window mullions, flutes, and molding coves were highlighted in white. A few pieces sported additional highlights of orange and black. Pine house paneling was also painted. (Because of an unfortunate trend toward a "natural" look, many of the Shore pieces have been stripped of their original color within the last 20 years.)

The basic construction technique for making the panel frame assemblies for furniture is identical to the technique used by house joiners when fabricating panels for house paneling. The beveled edges of the individual panels are fitted into grooves cut in the panel rails and stiles (horizontal and vertical framing). The rails and stiles are held together by mortise and tenon joints, which are pegged in place. The thumbnail molded beads which appear to be separate units surrounding the panels actually form integral parts of the rails and stiles. All sorts of variations in house paneling and furniture design can be achieved by shifting the type and location of a panel within the unit being built. In the resulting diversity of interpretations, some are more aesthetically pleasing than others.

Forms: presses and chests

Because of their rather large size, clothes presses are especially well adapted to raised-panel construction. (Clothes presses, both single-door and double-door varieties, are tall case pieces of furniture used for storing clothing. They served the same function as today's closet, a feature rare in early American architecture.) Most of these presses have shelves; but those originally without shelves have a peg rail for hanging coats and capes. This type of press, known as a hanger press, probably would have been placed in halls near entrance doors rather than in bedrooms. A sampling of early Shore records reveals that clothes presses enjoyed about 100 years of popularity, beginning in the second quarter of the 18th century.

While most of the blanket chests still encountered on the Eastern Shore belong to the plain, flat-board variety, the house joiners did construct raised-panel blanket chests using the same type panel frame assembly as in the clothes presses. The term "blanket chest" was not widely used, if at all, on the Shore in the 18th century: no specific mention of blanket chests has yet been found in any of the Shore wills and inventories surveyed by the author. Almost every inventory, however, lists at least one chest that is specifically distinguished from such similar items as a case of drawers, a chest of drawers, a case, or a trunk. Tools, books, clothes, and rags were among the goods stored in these chests, making it reasonable to assume that they were of the lift-lid, open-box form presently known as a blanket chest.

Cupboards, desks, and bookcases

Another type of raised-panel furniture found on the Shore is the flat-wall cupboard, characterized by cases with upper and lower cupboard sections, of which the upper section closure is glazed and the lower section is paneled. These pieces are freestanding, but they derive their design directly from the flush architectural cupboards found in many early Shore houses. Architectural cupboards are generally installed to fit snugly into fully paneled end walls, flanking fireplaces. The flat-wall cupboard was originally used to display decorative tableware and plate. No specific mention of flat-wall cupboards has yet been found in 18th-century wills and inventories, although the terms "cupboard" and "glazed cupboard" are common. One of these two categories evidently includes the flat-wall cupboard. Only a small number of flat-wall cupboards seems to have survived suggesting, perhaps, that the residents preferred the "built-in" architectural cupboard.

18th-century Eastern Shore inventories and wills occasionally mention bookcase/desks, today known as secretaries. Reference to bookcases alone only rarely occurs. It is therefore not surprising that freestanding bookcases are uncommon on the Shore; only three have been found. Sampled wills and inventories also suggest that the average person owned perhaps a Bible, a Book of Common Prayer, and a psalter, and therefore had no need for a freestanding bookcase to store so few books. Ownership of the freestanding raised-panel bookcase most likely was limited to those with a special need for keeping records, such as clerks of the country courts, or merchants. It is doubtful that the freestanding bookcase was made for domestic use. The three known surviving bookcases, tall with interiors fitted with a combination of shelves and vertical partitions, have double-door closures and a drawer arrangement across the base. The bookcases differ from the clothes presses, flat-wall cupboards, and blanket chests in that the bookcases all have solid board ends instead of the usual panel frame assembly.

The most unusual form of the Shore raised-panel furniture group is a type of corner cupboard known as the turkey-breast cupboard. The angular protrusion of the doors, similar to the sharp leading edge of a turkey's breast, is the source of this descriptive name. This arrangement increases the depth, and thus the capacity, of the cupboard without requiring additional wall

Yellow pine was invariably painted in colors that may seem garish today.

During the last 20 years, the prevalence of the fashionable "natural look" of bare wood encouraged many people to strip old pieces of their original paint. Eastern Shore raised-panel furniture, in particular, fell victim to this trend because the original painted finishes—usually bright blue or green with white, orange, and black highlights—were deemed gaudy by modern standards of taste. The yellow pine clothes press to the left, for example, was originally finished in typical bright green paint with white highlights when it was made ca 1760. Private Collection. The blanket chest below, constructed of yellow pine about 1790, sports blue and white paint. Blanket chests are not mentioned by name in old Eastern Shore records; but it is reasonable to assume that among the various types of "chests" listed in regional wills and inventories were examples of the lift-lid open box form illustrated here. House joiners employed the same sort of panel frame construction on the blanket chests that they used on the larger clothes presses. Private Collection.

> Because of their rather large size, clothes presses are especially well adapted to raised-panel construction.

space. Since the term "turkey-breast" has not been found in the Shore wills and inventories, it is assumed that the more generally cited "corner cupboard" or "cupboard" refers also to this form. Production of turkey-breast cupboards apparently was confined to the Delmarva Peninsula, with a good representation of this rare form found on Virginia's Eastern Shore. These cupboards were made from the second quarter of the 18th century into the first quarter of the 19th century, but few examples have been documented.

While the panel frame assembly is the same as that used for other raised-panel pieces, construction differences account for the diamond shape of turkey-breast cupboards. Such cupboards have a top board, generally a middle board, and a bottom board, each cut in an appropriate five-sided diamond shape. These boards are usually rebated into the vertical backboards and nailed into place. Shelves in the upper and lower cupboard sections provide added rigidity to the cupboard. The shelves

are rebated into the backboards and nailed in place. The front frame assembly, consisting of the two case stiles and the top, medial, and bottom rails, is then fitted and nailed to the piece. The front case stiles and the center backboard extend below the bottom of the case to support the cupboard. Most stiles have decorative bracket feet nailed to them.

Corner cupboards, frequently mentioned in Shore wills and inventories beginning in the second quarter of the 18th century, were a very popular form. Numerous corner cupboards of the raised-panel group have survived, most in the possession of Eastern Shore families. Constructed as single units, almost all of the corner cupboards are visually divided into upper and lower cupboard sections, generally separated by heavy waist bolection molding. The upper sections usually have glazed single-door closures; the lower cupboards, paneled single or double doors. The panel type and arrangement can vary considerably from cupboard to

Above left: Plate XXVI of William Salmon's *Palladio Londinensis.* Above: Plate XXIII of the same volume inspired the design of the clothes press on the facing page. Constructed of yellow pine 1740, this piece retains a blue and white finish similar to the paint with which it was originally decorated. It is classified as a hanger press because it is fitted with a peg rail for hanging coats and capes. The decorative paneling of the hanger press illustrated here was constructed by a technique well known to house joiners: beveled edges of the individual panels are fitted into grooves cut in the panel rails and stiles. These are held together by mortise and tenon joints, pegged in place. Photo of Salmon Plate XIII, courtesy the author. Hanger press, Private Collection.

cupboard. Unlike turkey-breast cupboards, corner cupboards almost always have returns or canted corners, often fitted with applied, highly decorative, fluted pilasters related to Salmon's designs. The case construction is identical to that of the turkey-breast cupboards, except that the top, middle, and bottom boards are cut into six-sided diamond shapes. ∎

Bermuda Furniture

Like much furniture of the American coastal mainland, pieces made in Bermuda were based on high-style English prototypes adapted to local materials and needs.

BY BETSY KENT

Bermuda first came to the attention of the British in 1609, when a ship bound for Jamestown, Virginia was wrecked on her reefs. The island, rich in fish and animal life, was subsequently used to provision Jamestown; and in 1612, a group of 60 hardy colonists were sent by the Virginia Company to settle there. By 1684, Bermuda had become a crown colony, sustained primarily by shipbuilding and trade.

Many of the island's earliest craftsmen learned their trades in the shipbuilding industry: cabinetmakers, joiners, and shipwrights or ship's carpenters were assisted by a full complement of apprentices. Richard Moore, for example, who was Bermuda's first appointed governor, had been a ship's carpenter. Examples of Bermuda furniture that exist today bear witness to the fact that these early craftsmen adapted their skills to the tasks at hand. The furniture they built is notable primarily for its simplicity and sturdiness, and for the aromatic *Juniperus Bermudiana*—island cedar—from which much of it is constructed.

Bermuda cedar is an especially rot-resistant wood, which does not warp like pine, or discolor and mildew like oak. It withstands the extreme and constant exposure to salt water and moist air that characterized most early Bermudian households. When the first shipwrecked sailors on the ill-fated vessel of 1609 explored the island, they found stands of this venerable wood. (Although some South Carolina furniture was constructed of native cedar, most furniture made in North America made use of other primary woods. Thus, it is easy to question the origins of a piece of "American" cedar furniture, and easier still to attribute it to Bermuda.) Cedar is a dense wood, and difficult to carve: this may have been a primary reason its use was not more

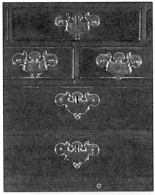

The characteristically simple and sturdy craftsmanship of Bermuda furniture is evident in the chest and highboy shown here. Opposite: 17th-century chest on frame. Note the onion feet, hooked-pattern skirt, and distinctive dovetailing of the joints. Private collection, photo Bermuda News Bureau. The cedar highboy, below and detail at left, displays the fine Chippendale style seen in some Bermuda furniture, indicating the prevailing English influence. The legs feature morning glory knee carving, wing scrolling and fine trifid feet. Note unusual scalloped frame apron, ca 1760. Courtesy the Bermuda National Trust; photos: Teddy Tucker.

widespread, although there are records indicating that cedar wood was shipped back to England from Bermuda. Thus, some pieces of cedar furniture have English origins.

History indicates that West Indian mahogany was imported to Bermuda during the 17th century. Like cedar, it had the redeeming quality of resistance to rot, and it was more easily carved into decorative furniture or household cabinetry detail. Pine and walnut came to the island from the eastern coast of the United States. It is also recorded that there was a fine stand of satinwood in Bermuda, but by the mid-17th century, most of it had been exported to England for use in furniture inlay. Not until the 19th century was there a class of Bermudians sufficiently large and affluent to patronize the makers of elaborately inlaid furniture; sturdier and simpler styles served the Bermuda householder's utilitarian purposes for nearly 200 years.

Few island pieces can be linked to the craftsmen who made them. The decorative dovetail joints embellishing the front corners of certain Bermuda chests are often thought to be craftsmen's "signatures," although no definitive attributions can be made. It is nevertheless tempting for a discerning observer to note that the newel-posts on certain Bermuda staircases are turned in a fashion similar to the ball-turned feet of a local 17th-century chest-on-frame.

Bermuda furniture forms

Predictably, the pieces that have survived in the greatest quantity from the 17th and 18th centuries are chairs, although there are examples of dining tables, high chests, and chests-on-frames known to have been made in Bermuda. Some of the chests-on-frames may well have been sea chests—a form that did not originate in Bermuda, but one that certainly contributed to the comfort of her seafaring populace. Just as conversation about the direction of the wind was taken seriously on this trade-based

island, so was the construction of a sailor's chest—possibly his primary possession during the long months of a voyage. One-third of Bermuda's men were always at sea earning a livelihood, or en route from one port to another. Between voyages, the sea chest was mounted on a frame to keep its contents dry. It became a useful piece of furniture, providing a flat surface at

Left: Bermuda cedar washstand, ca 1820, showing influence of the William and Mary style. Bermuda National Trust; photo Teddy Tucker. Below: Intricate dovetailing, thought to be the signature of Bermuda craftsmen, is seen here on an 18th century chest made of cedar. Bermuda National Trust, photo courtesy Bermuda News Bureau. Opposite: Cedar chair in the William and Mary style with Spanish feet and bannister back, ca. 1700. Courtesy the Bermuda National Trust; photos, Teddy Tucker.

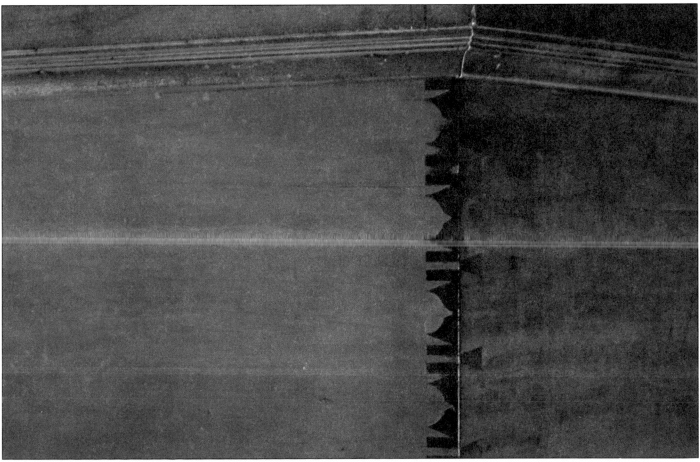

Bermuda furniture documents the island's rich history and gives testimony to the hardiness and taste of her early settlers.

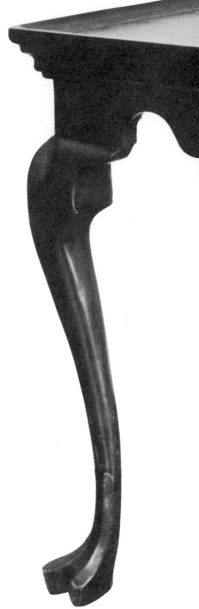

table level. Still other chests-on-frames may never have been to sea.

In some cases, cedar chests-on-frames were used to store the imported cones of hard sugar from the West Indies. In *Bermuda's Antique Furnishings*, Bryan Bordley Hyde states that this type of chest did not have a rounded top, nor did it have handles—but it did have a till. As to the construction of chests-on-frames, Colin Cooke and Sylvia Shorto, writing in *The Magazine Antiques* (August, 1979) point out that "boards used in chests and tables were frequently joined on the diagonal and most were secured by narrow strips of wood pinned to the unfinished side of the piece." These chests are often decorated with the subtle effects of delicate dovetail designs on the front corners. Frames for the earliest Bermuda chests had candlestick legs. Later examples, from the 18th century, had cabriole legs or squared-off straight legs in response to changing English styles.

Of course, because of the close diplomatic and trade relations between Bermuda and England, the influence of English furniture styles was bound to have an effect on pieces made in Bermuda. Imported pieces occasionally came over from England in very limited quantity during the early years. It must be remembered that early Bermuda was a working colony with few pretensions to elegance or a formal lifestyle. Although shipping was the life force of the island, furniture did not constitute a major category of trade. More important items needed to change hands: floor coverings, looking glasses, and brass appointments were

more likely to find a place in the cargo hold of a crowded ship. Even the hurricane shade—which by rights should have been an island invention to protect candles from the prevailing winds—was imported from England. The few pieces of furniture shipped over were apt to be covered and copied by local craftsmen. Obviously, English influence prevailed.

Indigenous examples

Examples of Bermuda furniture held in various public and private collections around the island demonstrate constructional and design characteristics that are typically Bermudian: decoratively cut dovetail joints, distinctively shaped aprons, well-turned legs, and onion feet. Verdmont, a pre-Georgian residence originally constructed between 1700 and 1710, is now a property of the Bermuda National Trust. It houses a significant collection of representative island work, providing a broad view of decades of indigenous craftsmanship. Among the early pieces at Verdmont are six William and Mary cedar chairs, examples of local work. Each has a board seat without cushion, eloquently expressing the no-nonsense lifestyle of the earliest colonists. These chairs have distinctive hand-turned knob finials, flat battens in the back support that differ from the split balusters more often found on American variations of this style of chair, and button feet. The back legs are without ornamentation.

Verdmont's parlor is graced by a cedar secretary in the Chippendale style, typical of the late 18th century (1760-1780) and representative of a number

This Bermuda cedar tray-top tea table in the Queen Anne style, ca 1740, is impeccably proportioned (27″ high, 38½″ wide and 22½″ deep) and is considered to be one of the finest examples of Bermudian furniture in existence. Notice the elegantly carved scalloped apron, the pinched apple leaf knees and the graceful sweep of the cabriole leg terminating in trifid or drake foot. The exquisite carving of this table is thought to have been influenced by the work of the Philadelphia furniture maker William Savery. Photo courtesy Bermuda News Bureau.

of functional island-made pieces of this type. It has bracket feet and English brasses, and the cedarwood has aged to a honey hue with a rich patina. Also of Bermuda origin are period Queen Anne style chairs of cedar, with slip seats that probably were reupholstered at a later date. The originals would most likely have been constructed of slate or woven palmetto bast. (The nature of more traditional cloth or horsehair upholstery is such that it provides a haven for the insects that thrive in Bermuda's constant dampness.) These chairs have a solid back splat, H stretchers and Dutch or club style feet.

Also at Verdmont is a Bermuda cedar gate-leg table, made around 1700, and reflecting the William and Mary style that was then fashionable in England. Its details of construction identify it positively as an island piece. (Not all the furniture at Verdmont was made on the island, of course. There is a particularly attractive English tilt top mahogany table, typical of the refined pieces of furniture that were brought in from England in the late 19th century, among them card tables and tea tables.)

A cedar highboy that may be seen in the Tucker House—another Bermuda National Trust property—illustrates a treatment that is characteristically Bermudian: the finished ball-and-claw feet at the rear of the piece are facing forward. No doubt this was to facilitate the flush placement of the highboy against a wall. Feet in this forward-facing position are called "marching feet," and they are seen on other locally made chests and side tables. Also in the Tucker house is a table measuring 35 inches across. That is the width of just one fine cedar board, giving some idea

Left: Bermuda cedar gateleg table, 1680-1700, is an exemplary piece and one of the few Bermudian gateleg tables known to exist. This piece is distinguished by the unusually close turnings of the legs. Like so many extant Bermudian pieces, this one reflects the William and Mary style fashionable in England at the time it was made. Private collection; photo courtesy the Bermuda News Bureau.

of the girth of virgin timber once so abundant on the island.

The St. George's Historical Society displays an Elizabethan-style trestle table that illustrates a mode of individualized carving, with strap work and scrolls. Its wide boards attest to its age; generally the wider the board, the older the piece of Bermuda furniture.

Over the years, indigenous furniture left Bermuda by one means or another. Some of it was sent back to England, as a letter written by Judge Hordesnell to the Secretary of the Lords of Trade and Plantations in 1687 attests:

> I have both my Selfe and others made inquiry for some good cedar plank which is not to be had of any considerable breadth but I have met with a very broad and large Ovill Table ye fayrest I ever see of cedar wch I am satisfied I intend to take aboard and bring with me, if it be too bigg, you may alter as you please.

Still other pieces, early on, found their way to America. Captain Sayle, for example, was an early governor of Bermuda who led a group of settlers to South Carolina. He transported all of his household furnishings in his own ship, and in the late 1600's, left a will in South Carolina with an inventory listing a number of cedar pieces.

In more recent times, with the advent of tourism to the island, American visitors have eagerly purchased Bermuda antique furniture to take home with them. In the United States today, it is sometimes confused with furniture made of cedar in such southern colonies as South Carolina. But Bermudians take great pride in their heritage and they are not people to let its tangible evidence slip easily from their hands. Although Bermuda's natural resources— her great stands of cedar and satinwood—were depleted early in her history, much of the fine early furniture made of native cedar remains on the island. In private collections and in public properties such as Verdmont, it documents the richness of Bermuda's history and gives testimony to the hardiness and taste of her early settlers. ∎

The Fiddleback Chair

Chairmakers in New York, New Jersey, and New England adapted the Queen Anne style to the turned chair tradition, creating the ubiquitous fiddleback.

BY KATHLEEN EAGEN JOHNSON

The fiddleback chair, that functional piece of early American furniture, demonstrates the cultural interaction among craftsmen working in New York, New Jersey, and New England who adapted the chair's basic form to suit distinct regional preferences. Proportions of the chair, as well as the type and execution of its turnings varied from region to region, attesting to the widespread appeal of the fiddleback style. The chairs enjoyed a large and diverse market among late 18th- and early 19th-century families from many different economic and ethnic backgrounds.

The fiddleback chair, also called "rush bottom" or "York," is a Queen Anne-style turned chair, usually painted black or reddish brown, with a rush seat. The term "York" was used primarily in Connecticut in reference to the New York origin of the form. Because the survival of documentary materials has been spotty, the origins of the fiddleback are cloudy. Most probably, a now unknown New York City chairmaker developed the style around 1750. The earliest presently known reference to a fiddleback chair comes from Connecticut. Benno Forman, the noted American furniture expert, found "6 New Fashion york chairs" in the 1757 inventory of Joseph Blackleach of Stratford. Such chairs continued to be made well into the 19th century.

The fiddleback chair is not an expression of naive vision and inferior woodworking skills, as some might think. On the contrary, it is an intentional translation of the elements of the carved mahogany or walnut, cabriole legged, Queen Anne-style chair into the vocabulary of the turned chair tradition. The chairmaker who conceived of the fiddleback chair thoroughly understood the aesthetics of the Queen Anne style and adapted them to his craft.

One excellent example of the early fiddleback style is a chair branded by David Coutant, a maker of rush bottom and Windsor chairs, who worked in New Rochelle and New York City. Coutant realized the complexity of the form: at its best his fiddleback features bold, well-proportioned turnings on the rear stiles, legs, and tripartite front stretcher; a curved crest rail; and broad splat.

Some turners took shortcuts in fiddleback chair production. On cheaper chairs the legs extend above the rush seat; on finer chairs the legs are crafted to meet the chamfered corners of the front seat rail. For people who could not afford finely turned chairs and for those who hankered to own chairs in the fiddleback style but did not care about quality, a number of craftsmen created chairs of similar design but with poor proportions and turnings; they sometimes employed soft, cheap woods like pine for the turned legs and stiles.

Contrary to popular misconception, despite its origins in the once-Dutch colony of New York, the fiddleback is not purely Dutch in style. Although the vase and ball turnings on the middle of its rear stiles are "borrowed" from chairs made in the European lowland countries and in New York and New Jersey, the fiddleback's distinctive legs are actually inspired by English country turning as exemplified by chairs made in East Anglia and Lancashire. The front stretcher and overall design of its rear stiles relates closely to those elements in William and Mary style chairs constructed in Boston. Merchants shipped these leather chairs to New York and other colonies; the fiddleback creator probably copied his front stretcher from a Boston chair or a New York rendition of the Boston prototype.

The popularity of the fiddleback chair extended well beyond the boundaries of what is now New York City. As the style spread to other regions, local

This page: Late 18th-century, rush-seated chair of maple, pine, and hickory, branded by New York maker David Coutant. Sleepy Hollow Restorations, Tarrytown, New York. Fiddleback chairs were made from about 1750 until the mid-19th century. Their skillfully woven rush seats were a comfortable alternative to upholstered seating during warm weather.

93

craftsmen of different ethnic groups created their own versions of the fiddleback. Some of these beautifully conceived, well-executed experiments rose above the status of the common chair. But as time went by, most knock-offs grew shoddy. The ideal fiddleback design became debased as far as proportions and quality of turning were concerned.

Fiddleback chairs are traditionally associated with the Hudson Valley, yet it seems likely that many fiddlebacks used in the Valley were shipped up-river from New York City. Chairs branded by New York City chairmakers can be traced to families like the Lansings and the Van Vlecks who resided in the northern end of the Valley. Many unmarked chairs no doubt found their way north, as well.

At least one Hudson Valley chairmaker produced imitations. At the turn of the 19th century, James Chestney advertised in the *Albany Gazette* that he sold a variety of chairs—including fiddlebacks—at his chair manufactory. A woodcut of slatback, fiddleback, and Windsor chairs illustrates his still extant advertisement.

Nor were fiddlebacks strangers to Long Island. In *Long Island is My Nation*, Dean Failey notes that the term "fiddleback" was used on the Island as early as 1784, when it is mentioned in the account book of John Paine, a Southold joiner. Between the years 1796 and 1808, Nathaniel Dominy, the Oyster Bay jack-of-all-trades, listed 31 fiddleback chairs in his accounts. Chairs made on Long Island had more in common stylistically with the Connecticut adaptation of the style than with the original New York type.

New England turners created their own brand of York chairs and freely improvised upon the New York fiddleback. As far up the Connecticut Valley as Deerfield, Massachusetts, chairmakers produced variations of the York chair. The Durand family of turners in Milford, Connecticut recorded such chairs in their account book from the early 1760s to 1818. At first their style aped the New York fiddleback rather closely, with slight variations in the choice and execution of turnings. But by varying crest rails, splats, and turnings, the Durands and neighboring craftsmen used the basic form of the york chair as a springboard for individual design talent. Robert Trent's study of coastal Connecticut turned chairs, entitled *Hearts and Crowns*, outlines the paths these improvisors took.

Fiddlebacks appeared elsewhere in New England. Rhode Island specimens of the chair have feet that are more horizontally aligned, and distinctive, circular cutouts at the ends of the crest rails. These cutouts are also seen on walnut chairs of Rhode Island origin, according to Patricia Kane, curator of American decorative arts at Yale University Art Gallery. It seems clear that ideas as well as goods were actively traded between Rhode Island and the New York towns across Long Island Sound.

New Jersey chairs are equally distinctive. They display the suggestion of a "saddle" at the top of the crest rail, a tapering of the lower rail, and a flattened ball turning between the lower and seat rails on the rear stiles. New Jersey chairs also exhibit a swelling in the center of some front stretchers—as seen in Pennsylvania chairs—and other characteristics more in keeping with Delaware Valley chairs than with the original New York fiddlebacks.

Since many have survived, the fiddleback chair must have been a familiar object, especially to New Yorkers. Probate inventories—the listing of property made upon the death of a head of household—attest the chair's popularity among various ethnic groups. In modest homes they ranked as the only or the best chairs suitable for display in the parlor. The Van Rensselaers, Beekmans, and other members of New York's upper class probably used these chairs in lesser rooms. Since late 18th- and early 19th-century Americans avoided upholstered furniture in the summer, unless it was slipcovered, fiddlebacks and other rush bottom chairs must have been held in high esteem for seating during the hot months. The 1807 inventory of Leopold Beck listed 14 mahogany chairs upholstered in horsehair and valued at 16 shillings each; 7 old common chairs at 1 shilling,

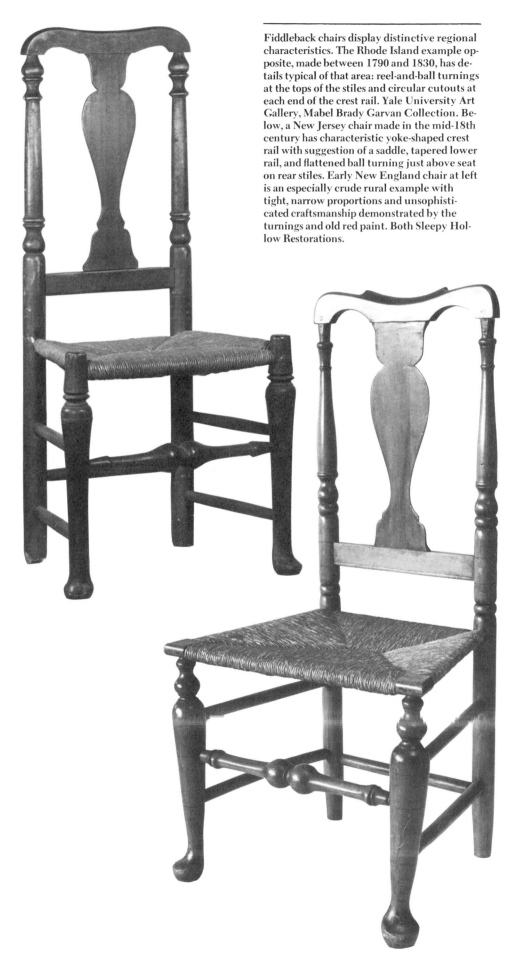

Fiddleback chairs display distinctive regional characteristics. The Rhode Island example opposite, made between 1790 and 1830, has details typical of that area: reel-and-ball turnings at the tops of the stiles and circular cutouts at each end of the crest rail. Yale University Art Gallery, Mabel Brady Garvan Collection. Below, a New Jersey chair made in the mid-18th century has characteristic yoke-shaped crest rail with suggestion of a saddle, tapered lower rail, and flattened ball turning just above seat on rear stiles. Early New England chair at left is an especially crude rural example with tight, narrow proportions and unsophisticated craftsmanship demonstrated by the turnings and old red paint. Both Sleepy Hollow Restorations.

95

6 pence apiece; and "6 common chairs (fiddleback'd)" at 5 shillings each, suggesting that in his household, and no doubt in many others, fiddlebacks were middling sorts of chairs. This type of turned chair shared roughly the same status as its siblings the windsor, the slatback, and the bannisterback.

The venerable Mrs. Isaac Day of Ithaca, New York thought enough of her fiddleback to have her portrait painted while seated in it. Born in 1767, she came to Ithaca from Vermont in 1809 with her husband, who headed a school. Henry Walton, a local artist, painted Mrs. Day in 1846, the year of her death.

Even George Washington owned a fiddleback armchair which he used during the New York campaign in the Revolutionary War. Made for him by Jacob Smith, a New York City turner who registered as a freeman in 1762 and later headed a contingent of makers of

Individual Connecticut turners varied the details of the basic New York fiddleback chair, creating unique improvisations. This early 18th-century example, carefully crafted of maple, pine and hickory, has horizontally scrolled arms typically found on Connecticut fiddleback armchairs. Sturdy trumpet-turned legs terminate in large toed-out, pad-on-disc feet. Sleepy Hollow Restorations.

rush bottom chairs in a parade honoring the Constitution in 1788, this magnificently turned chair of huge proportions is in the collection of Washington's headquarters in the Purdy house in White Plains, New York.

The fiddleback chair was so popular that versions of it were reproduced during the so-called Colonial Revival of the late 19th and early 20th centuries. At that time, its origins in the 18th century and its production into the 19th century were overlooked. Esther Singleton, a pioneering writer in the fields of New York social history and decorative arts, published a picture of a fiddleback chair in *Furniture of Our Forefathers* (1901) which she thought had belonged to Annetje Jans, one of New Netherlands' earliest female settlers. Even though Jans, who arrived in the colony in 1630, holds legendary status in the annals of New York history, she could not have possibly owned a fiddleback chair! At least one furniture company created its own colonial revival york chair with thickly rectangular seat rails and lifeless turnings. These revival chairs are sometimes mistaken for the originals. Not all early 20th-century statements about fiddleback chairs are misleading or false: in a 1906 edition of Washington Irving's *The Legend of Sleepy Hollow*, the illustrator Arthur Keller depicted Ichabod Crane seated in a fiddleback chair reflecting upon the ghost stories he has just heard. Keller's choice of this style chair is logical and appropriate since the story is set in early 19th-century Tarrytown, New York.

Misconceptions have grown up around the fiddleback chair. Despite the fact that the style almost certainly originated in the urban center of New York and continued to be made there, many people believe that these chairs developed in the Hudson Valley because of the numbers found there. Many of these were in fact imported from New York City. Moreover, fiddlebacks were made far later than traditionally thought, illustrating how inaccurate art historical timelines can be.

These chairs are not entirely Dutch in inspiration; they also draw heavily

Fiddlebacks are not entirely Dutch in inspiration; they draw heavily on the turning traditions of England and New England.

Crafted in maple between 1730 and 1740, the prototypical chair at left is the handiwork of an anonymous New York maker. Note the pleasing proportions of the violin-shaped splat or "fiddleback," the yoke crest, and trumpet legs with disc pad feet. It retains an even layer of old black paint. Courtesy Israel Sack, Inc., New York.

on English and New England turning traditions. Not solely a New York phenomenon, adaptations of the chair flourished in Connecticut, Massachusetts, Rhode Island, and New Jersey. Examination of the existing documentation on this ubiquitous chair, and comparisons of construction and style among the surviving fiddlebacks dispels these misconceptions and provides a more accurate history. ∎

A precursor of the American fiddleback, the English ladderback turned chair at left was made of cherrywood in East Anglia between 1610 and 1750. Yale University Art Gallery, the Mabel Brady Garvan Collection. Another predecessor was the transitional William and Mary/Queen Anne leatherback turned chair like the example above, which was probably made in Boston toward the close of the 17th century. Note turnings on rear stiles. Sleepy Hollow Restorations.

The Rocking Chair

The earliest rockers were probably adaptations of standard chairs, but by the mid-19th century, they were a standard form in the furniture-maker's repertory.

BY RUTH MILLER FITZGIBBONS

The earliest rocking chairs were actually adaptations of other chairs. That is, they were originally stationary, straight-legged chairs, to which rockers were subsequently attached. Not only were these early conversions often clumsy, but some alteration of the chair was necessary to accomplish the adaptation. This often entailed cutting the chair legs down, or employing some unsightly bolting device, adaptations that antiquarians do not favor.

Even beyond this esthetic concern, there is also a prevailing snobbery toward the rocking chair, and even toward the act of rocking itself. Antiquarian Wallace Nutting wrote, in expressing his belief that all Windsor rockers were conversions, "As it is no longer good form to rock, and for that matter never could have been, we need not grieve over the false Windsor rocker, except to regret that so many thousands of good Windsors have been

slat-back

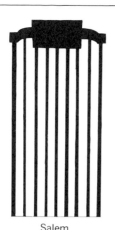

Salem

splat-back

comb-back

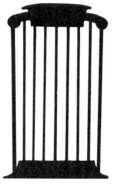

Sheraton "fancy chair"

Boston

fiddle-back

bannister-back

Drawings by Richard Zoerher

spoiled by adding rockers."

Apparently, the disdain for rocking chairs extended into the genteel circles of England. British author Harriet Martineau wrote, upon her return from the United States in 1836, "The disagreeable practice of rocking in the chair . . . how this lazy and ungraceful indulgence ever became general, I cannot imagine, but the [American] nation seems so wedded to it, that I see little chance of its being forsaken."

The origin: popular myths and conjectures

Though a good number of notions about the origin of the rocking chair have been debated, there is no disagreement over the fact that some type of arc-shaped runners were attached to cradles as far back as the 14th century in Europe. The word "rocker" originally referred to the nurse who took charge of rocking the infants to sleep, which may explain why several historians have written that the earliest rocking chairs were called "nurse's chairs" by some. Thereafter, "rocker" was associated with the cradle's base.

Precisely who had the bright idea of adapting rockers to a chair is not known. In any case, nothing substantial has been written about rockers, and/or this debate, for decades. Prior to 1948, it was almost universally accepted that

the inventor was an American. Since then, there has been evidence of a rocking chair in England, believed to date from the early 1600s. It seems that a toy rocking chair, measuring only three and a half inches high, was unearthed in a London plague pit from the reign of Charles I. Given this evidence, and conceding that an occasional European may have seen fit to attach cradle rockers to a chair, it is possible that the idea of the rocking chair is not indigenous to America. However, the practice was never widespread in Europe (nor is it to this day), and most rocking chairs to be found abroad are still referred to as "American rockers."

That aside, it still remains a mystery as to what American began the practice of converting chairs to rockers. Esther Stevens Fraser, co-author with Walter A. Dyer of *The Rocking Chair: An American Institution* (The Century

Opposite page: Bow-back Windsor rocking armchair with comb, c. 1800-1810. At the turn of the 18th century rocking chairs became increasingly popular in America and, since not many were being produced, chair owners often converted their chairs into rockers. Such is the case with this Windsor. The rockers themselves distinguish this as a converted rocker. They extend an equal distance beyond the front and rear legs of the chair and are identical in shape at each end—like the rockers on cradles—designed to be perfectly balanced at mid-point to prevent an upset. True rockers were longer in back than in front. Photo courtesy Old Sturbridge Village.

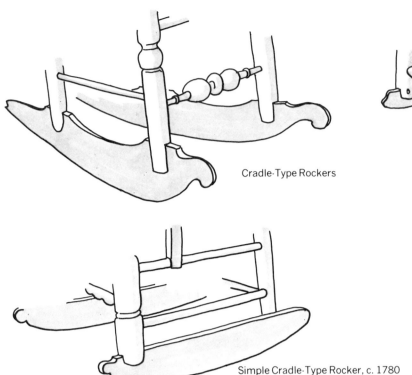

Cradle-Type Rockers

Simple Cradle-Type Rocker, c. 1780

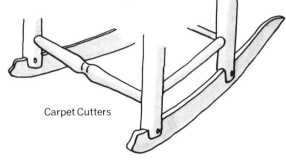

Carpet Cutters

Types of Rockers

No single development in the rocker can account for the evolution of style. However, most early rockers—such as two of those shown left—share a common characteristic: they are rough imitations of the rockers on baby cradles—hence the name, cradle rockers. The "carpet cutter" rocker illustrated here has been set into a notch in the leg and bolted to it for added strength.

Co., New York & London, 1928), offers some engaging suggestions. With guileless logic, she states, "We feel certain that some American *man* invented the rocking chair for his personal use. Why? Because the menfolk are particularly partial to rockers."

The American man that myth would have us believe did the inventing was none other than Benjamin Franklin. Ms. Fraser has tried valiantly to substantiate the rumor by searching in Franklin's documents and in accounts of his contemporaries for some evidence linking Franklin to the development of the rocking chair. The evidence, other authorities agree, is nonexistent. Although there are references that indicate that Franklin owned a "great arm chair with rockers" as early as 1787, the chronicles don't substantiate the theory that it was of his own device.

As early as 1762, however, there are existing records of rocking chairs being sold or repaired in various parts of the country. Eliakim Smith, a cabinetmaker residing in Hadley, Massachusetts, left a ledger to that effect, as did a craftsman in Middletown, Pennsylvania, in 1766, and Philadelphia's renowned cabinetmaker William Savery in 1774. Whether there were rocking chairs in use any earlier, as some historians suspect, remains a matter of conjecture.

The early styles

Walter Dyer has written, "The layman will be chiefly interested in knowing that a very old converted rocking chair may date back to the middle of the 18th century, but was more probably converted after the revolution." It is fairly simple to surmise how these early con-

verted rocking chairs may have come to be. Some were transformed by craftsmen, as evidenced by the aforementioned records. Still more, it is suspected, were the work of amateurs who whittled rockers from boards or wood pieces that happened to be handy. A chair whose legs had succumbed to wear, perhaps one that was 50 years old or more, may have been a likely candidate for conversion. Says Dyer, "Obviously, there was no rule as to how old or new a chair should be converted, provided it was sound enough to warrant the trouble."

Early slat-backed chairs, which were favored for their sturdy proportions and comfort, are the earliest chairs found with applied rockers. In addition, bannister-back, fiddle-back, later slat-back, and early Windsors appear with rockers affixed. Although these chairs have a rather makeshift appearance, they are—because of their age and rarity—the most valuable to collectors.

The "true" rocking chair, or one that was intended as such from its inception, came into being sometime between 1790 and 1800, though the practice of converting chairs continued for some 50 years thereafter. Most authorities agree that the earliest designs for true rockers were somewhat clumsy both esthetically and in execution. "No master craftsman such as Chippendale or Hepplewhite had published any designs for rocking chairs whereby the American craftsman could be guided," allows Fraser.

The early true rockers shared the characteristics of the Sheraton "fancy" and the Windsor chairs, because these were the shops that first began to produce them. From there on, the evolution of the rocking chair followed somewhat that of American furniture in general, reflecting influences of the Empire style, when it was in vogue, and embracing with enthusiasm the decorations of the bronze stenciling era, which was popular up until the Victorian period. Alterations on basic styles, however, changed very little in the early decades of the 19th century. Dyer remarks in an article in a 1928 issue of *House & Garden,* "It is possible to find odd chairs . . . which illustrate a departure from the main current of style development" in the outlying reaches of New England. But in the main, the chairs evolved slowly until the advent of the Civil War, after which more massive upholstered and scroll-armed styles came to the fore.

Since the addition of the rockers themselves added three to five inches in

height, as well as a visual weight at the chair's base, it was up to the individual craftsman to alter the line and proportion of the chair style accordingly. This may account for the fact that the more pleasing rocking chairs have arms and high backs for esthetic balance.

Above: Boston rocker, New England, 1830s. Maple and pine; painted, grained, and stenciled. This is a typical Boston rocker: rolled seat, rolling crest, and turned legs. Courtesy Essex Institute, Salem, Mass.

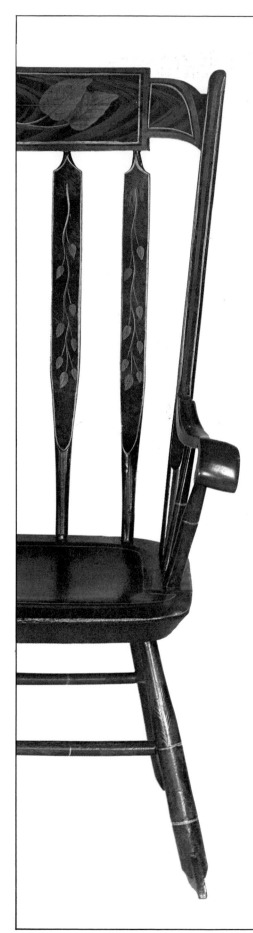

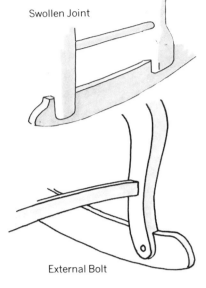

Swollen Joint

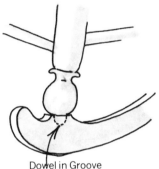

External Bolt

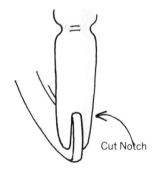

Dowel in Groove

Cut Notch

It is fairly easy for the informed collector to detect the difference between a converted rocker and an authentic or true one. Some telltale signs are outlined in the accompanying diagrams.

Shapes of rockers, methods of joining

If it were possible to trace accurately the evolution of the shape and construction of the rocker appendages themselves, it would facilitate the process of dating and placing early rocking chairs. No such chronology exists, partly because cabinetmakers of the day worked independently of one another. No single development can account for the evolution of style. There are, however, some general characteristics they all shared.

Most early rockers were either rough imitations of cradle rockers, or thin slats fit into cutouts or grooves in the chair legs. The former followed the bulky thickness of cradle rockers, with rather crude shaping along the top line. These often had holes in the center, to which doweled extensions of the chair's legs were inserted and secured with a wood pin at the joint.

The thin, slatlike rockers, called "carpet cutters," or "knife-blade" rockers, were set into notches cut from the legs. Still other rockers, of varying widths and shapes, were simply bolted

Left: Arrow-back Windsor rocking chair, Maine, c. 1830. Maple and pine, 41″ high. Private collection. Opposite page: Arrow-back Windsor rocking chair, New England, 1820s; 44″ high. Courtesy Burton and Helaine Fendelman. Painted decoration added to the popularity of Windsor chairs and rockers. The example at left is painted with stylized leaves; oak leaves and acorns decorate the yellow rocker.

Methods of Joining Rockers

Above from the top: If the carpenter went to the trouble of swelling the joint—enlarging the wood pieces to add stability to the chair—you can be certain that the chair was originally constructed as a rocker. Other rockers of varying widths were bolted to the outside of the chair leg (external bolt), or the leg was fitted into a groove in the rocker for the dowel and groove joint. Also, notches were cut from either the inner, outer, or middle of the leg (as shown here) to join thin slat-like "carpet cutter" or "knife blade" rockers to the chair leg.

"The most popular chair ever made, which people sit in, antiquarians despise, and novices seek"—the Boston rocker.

onto the outside of the chair leg, or fitted into what are termed "swollen joints"—enlarged wood pieces at the joint which add stability to the chair. Later, the wider rockers were adorned with an interesting variety of stenciled decorations.

A common trait of the earliest rockers is an extension of equal distance beyond the front and rear legs. The two ends being shaped identically, when viewed from the side, the silhouette appears perfectly symmetrical.

Sometime between 1810 and 1815, according to Fraser and Dyer, the back of the rocker was extended some four to ten inches. They write, "Someone had discovered that a wonderful swing could be gained by means of increased length, and the bumped ankles and bruised insteps that it would cause were not considered." The authors suggest that the greater the rear extension, the later the date of the chair. But they caution against applying this theory as a hard-and-fast rule. Sometimes old and new techniques overlapped, especially in the more remote locations.

Celebrated styles: the Boston, the Salem, the Shaker

Windsor rockers were the forerunners of a type that would come to be the most widely used and beloved rocking chairs of all time—save perhaps Michael Thonet's fluid bentwood design. The Boston rocker was once described by Wallace Nutting as "the most popular chair ever made, which people sit in, antiquarians despise, and novices seek." Because there are a number of Boston rockers still around today

they are quite reasonably priced, thus ideal for modest collectors.

Boston rockers were first produced in 1825 and continued to be made for 40 years. After 1840 they were assembled by machine. The derivation of the name is a mystery, as most authorities suspect they were originally developed in Connecticut. To add confusion, many people in the 19th century referred to *all* rockers as Boston rockers.

The Boston rocker is distinctive. Its most telling characteristic is a pronounced rolling seat, sloped front and back. (The seat curve was accomplished most often in pine, though the rest of the chair was constructed chiefly of maple.) The stretchers and legs are turned, and the legs are raked—turned outward slightly at an angle from the seat. The rockers are normally flat, attached by a doweled extension of the leg. Gently sloping arms reiterate the curve of the seat, extremities being curved to accommodate the hands. The back of the Boston consists of two stiles with seven slender spindles in between, although there are variations substituting a slat back. The crest rail was often a flat horizontal, or cut out to outline the shape of the head, and in some instances, finished with scrolled sides.

But it was the painted decoration on the Boston rocker that made it appealing to those who favored the "fancy" style. Most of the decorations followed the conventional New England fruit and flower motifs, but occasionally a decorator would deviate from the norm with patriotic figures or rural landscapes. The more elaborate the painting or stenciling, the higher the value of the chair.

A country cousin of the Boston rocker, and a style often confused with

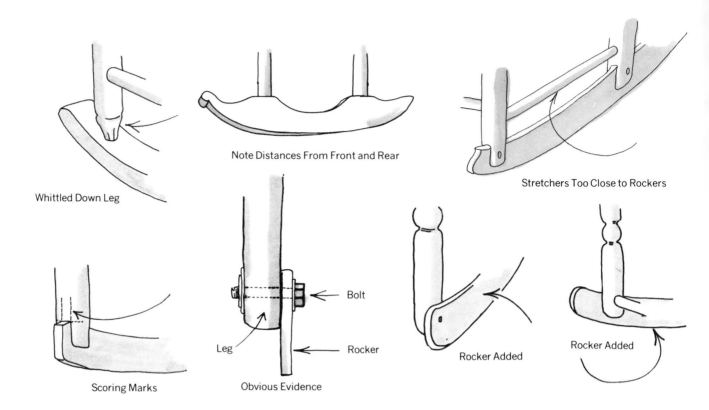

Whittled Down Leg

Note Distances From Front and Rear

Stretchers Too Close to Rockers

Scoring Marks

Obvious Evidence

Leg

Bolt

Rocker

Rocker Added

Rocker Added

1. Compare finishes and layers of paint.
Are there differences between the rockers and the chair itself?

2. Compare types and qualities of wood.
Are they different? Most conversions have rockers of a lesser or more pliable grade of wood.

3. Have the legs been modified?
Are they whittled down? Are there scoring marks on the legs indicating the depth of the slot to be cut for rockers?

4. Have the legs been designed with a tapered dowel base?
Or is the width at the bottom deliberately widened to accommodate a rocker? These are true rockers.

5. Look at the length and shape of the rockers themselves.
Early converted rockers extended an equal distance beyond the front and rear legs.

6. Are there side stretchers?
Side stretchers often indicate a converted chair. However, it took a while for cabinetmakers to learn that side stretchers weren't necessary for stability, so some true rockers have them too.

7. Where are the stretchers located?
Are they too close to the rockers to have been designed that way?

8. Is there blatant evidence of rockers having been added?
Some rockers were simply bolted onto the outside or inside of the chair's legs.

9. What is the style of the chair?
If the chair predates 1800, chances are it is a converted rocker. However, because of the uncertainty surrounding the origin of these early rockers, you can't be sure.

10. Does the style of the chair antedate that of the rocker?
If the chair itself seems to be much older than the style of rocker indicates (remember, the later ones were usually extended four to ten inches beyond the rear leg), it was probably converted.

it, is the Salem rocker. Also derived from a Windsor, the Salem has two chief differences from the Boston. Its seat is more of a saddle or a flat shape; and its crest rail was more shaped and more elaborately decorated.

"If the Shakers had been in the chair business 50 years earlier," writes Fraser, "they would have invented the rocking chair." John G. Shea, author of *Antique Country Furniture of North America* (Van Nostrand Reinhold Company, New York, 1975), contends that "while they cannot be credited with 'inventing' the rocking chair, the Shakers did more to develop its design and promote its use than any other chairmakers."

The Shakers adapted their familiar ladder-back style to rockers that were measured and shaped to fit the human body. According to Shea, the Shakers took pains to experiment with proportions and dimensions until they hit upon exactly the right formula to house the human body in comfort. Shaker seats were normally cane, with rockers of the thin carpet-cutter type.

It is extremely difficult today to find rocking chairs that predate 1800. Those produced between 1800 and 1810 are also scarce but well worthy of the collector's eye, as they are often more graceful than later models. Most rocking chairs on the antiques circuit today were made after 1830. Dealers advise the novice collector to start with mid-century illustrations to and work backward.

One final word in relation to collecting rockers: Dealers warn that there are numerous fakes circulating, it being a popular chair for imitation during the 1920s. Collectors are advised to make these purchases only at the most repu-table dealers or at auctions where authenticity is guaranteed.

The story of the rocking chair portrays some of the most appealing traits of our Yankee forebears. The way in which such a novel notion spread is testimony to the ingenuity of this sturdy folk. Its soothing virtues—comfort and stability—are as valid today as when great-grandma sat and knit by the fire.■

Shaker slat-back rocker, New England, 1830s; maple. Shaker rockers, as exemplified here, display simple lines, a lack of elaborate turnings and, often, mushroom-shaped knobs where the arm and leg-post join. Courtesy **Bernard S. and Dean Levy, Inc., New York.**

Painted Furniture

Free-brush painting, stenciling, and Japanning were popular techniques for decorating furniture in America.

BY RUTH MILLER FITZGIBBONS

In 1977 the Renwick Gallery, an off-shoot of the Smithsonian Institution in Washington, D.C., mounted an ambitious exhibition entitled "Paint on Wood: Decorated American Furniture Since the 17th Century." The show was pure visual delight—an inspiring array of vivid colors and fanciful folk artistry as well as high style and town furniture. However, the exhibition was significant for reasons other than its vigor and style. The objects assembled, spanning four centuries of furniture styles, pro-

vided an illuminating history of American furniture design. Painted furniture, it seems, has been a pervasive force in furniture design since the late 1600s, with origins as diverse as the immigrant population, and with a heritage as rich as any native art.

It may be surprising to learn that the first application of paint in this country was on furniture, where, as one collector put it, a little pigment could stretch a long way. Pigments were hard to come by. Nevertheless, almost all the early oak furniture crafted by America's first settlers originally was painted or stained. According to Lloyd E. Herman, director of the Renwick Gallery, "both carved and uncarved pieces were frequently decorated, as well, with boldly applied painted designs." Paint

Painted decoration brightened country furniture and added elegance to high-style city pieces.

Brightly painted decoration has always been a part of America's furniture-making tradition. At the close of the Revolutionary War, furniture painting blossomed into a full-blown industry that would span the Federal period and continue through the rise of the immensely popular "fancy" furniture. Opposite page, top: Tall clock, probably Schuylkill, Pennsylvania, early 19th century. Courtesy Philadelphia Museum of Art, Titus C. Geesey Collection. Opposite page, below: Detail from chest, 1834. Courtesy Winterthur Museum. Left: Drawings showing popular decorative designs from the Guilford-Saybrook area of Connecticut. Below: Pine chest, probably Berks county, late 18th century. Courtesy Winterthur Museum.

not only lent an artistic quality to the colonists' handiwork, but also was a means of protecting and preserving the wood.

The binding properties of early paints and stains were not very durable. But the reason decoration on most of the earliest furniture pieces has not lasted is related more to the feverish scrapings of 19th-century collectors and those of subsequent generations in search of the "natural" wood, than to erosion. A collector is lucky to happen

upon a painted survivor that predates 1700.

Historians have placed the earliest decorated furniture in the Connecticut River valley. "From the luxuriant valley farms near the mouth of the Connecticut River, came many interesting painted highboys, chests, and boxes," writes historian Jean Lipman in her book *American Folk Decoration.* "These pieces, though somewhat reminiscent of Dutch, Flemish, or French decoration, and especially of English

crewelwork, have a distinctly American . . . simplicity of design," she adds. The area around Hadley, Massachusetts was particularly fruitful. Over 150 delicately painted "Hadley chests," dating from 1670 to 1730, still exist today.

Nearby, in the neighboring Dutch settlements along the Hudson River valley, painting became popular as a means of decorating large cupboards called *kas* (which is pronounced "kass"). Other rural regions in New

107

Painted decoration brightened country furniture and added elegance to high-style city pieces.

England, New York, New Jersey, and Pennsylvania also adopted the custom of applying painted decoration to their furniture designs.

Elaborately ornamented furniture in the tradition of *chinoiserie* began to be produced in the urban centers of New York and Boston shortly after 1700, even though painted furniture remained largely a rural craft up until the Revolutionary War. Master craftsmen, including Chippendale, published design pattern books extolling the virtues of a painting technique called *japanning*, which simulates oriental lacquered furniture. City artisans turned out costly and highly styled japanned furniture that was far removed from its country counterpart.

With the exception of japanning, the practice of painted decoration was all but dormant for a time just prior to the Revolution, when carved ornament was in vogue, and paint used merely as an embellishment for the wood detail. But with the close of the war, furniture painting blossomed into a full-blown industry that would span the Federal period (from 1788 to 1820) and continue through the rise of the immensely popular "fancy" furniture, which was at its peak around 1820. According to Robert Bishop, director of the Museum of American Folk Art in New York, the fashion was precipitated by the many French craftsmen who came to America toward the end of the 1700s and used stencil and gilt decoration to imitate the French taste for ormulu. In addition, from this time on, the growth of "factory" production (furniture craftshops with as few as two or three employees) somewhat altered the methods of decoration. Bronze stenciling became a convenient and expedient means of applying decoration to furniture, and though there are examples of freehand painted decoration through-

out the 19th century (and, much later, in reproduction antiques), stenciling all but supplanted the earlier freehand brushstroke mode.

Pigments and paints

For those of us accustomed to the convenience of ordering canned paints in virtually any color desired, it is difficult to imagine what it would be like to commence a project without it. Premixed paints were not available to furniture decorators until well into the 1800s. The early painter-stainers, both professional and amateur, had to rely on pigments from the earth or metals, or on imports from England. Earth pigments, such as iron oxide or ochre, were dug in the form of clay, then washed with water, and, if they were to be

mixed with oil, left to dry. Then the pigment was ground in linseed or nut oil in a primitively fashioned grinder. The preparation of oil paints was a costly affair, especially if the decorator favored the highly taxed but more varied pigments from England.

A less expensive but far less durable alternative was distemper paint, which substituted hot water and glue size (a glutenous material) for the oil. And after 1800, still another base—buttermilk sometimes mixed with blood to make a dark, country finish—was used, in a revival of casein paints (an ancient process rendered obsolete in the 15th century by the discovery of oil-based paints).

The most frequently used colors during the 17th century were black and

red, as these were the most readily accessible and easily processed pigments. Blue and green were also available from metals and verdigris, the latter forming the basis of a green paint provided by tarnished copper. Various gradations of white, taken from the pigment in white lead, were popular background and filler colors.

In the 18th century, when paint first became popular in the United States for use on interior and exterior walls, more paint colors became available. According to Dean Fales—whose book *Painted American Furniture* is a most complete and fascinating resource—an advertisement in *The New England Journal*, dated 1723, offered some 30 colors for sale, including "white and red lead, Indian Red and Spanish

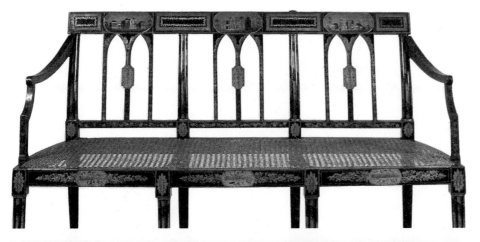

Above: Two views of a settee attributed to John and Hugh Findlay, 1805. Courtesy The Baltimore Museum of Art. Vignetted on this black-and-gilt Sheraton settee are three Baltimore landmarks including (detail) an early bank building. Below: Detail of serving table, ca 1828. Collection of Jack F. Fensternmacher. Striped, grained, and marbleized effects are created through skillful application of paint.

brown, Spanish white, spruce yellow, vermillion, ruddle, smalt, and umber . . . for oyl or water." (Ruddle is a red ochre color and smalt is deep blue.)

Have brush, will travel

The decorators of early painted furniture were probably the same craftsmen who carved and built the furniture itself. (Again, early japanned pieces are the exception because in most cases the decorator was not the cabinetmaker.) Some collectors find the harmony of form and ornament most pleasing in these early pieces, which were both constructed and decorated by the same craftsman. Sometime around 1750, professionally trained painter-stainers, whose job it was to mix paints, refine oil, and make brushes, in addition to plying their art, began to specialize in furniture painting. From then on, the furniture makers, or joiners, as they were called, left the finishing of their pieces to skilled artists.

We know very little about these early decorators, since there is often nothing more than a favored pattern or motif to identify them with their work. It is believed that most were itinerant artists who traveled from place to place, working for their bed and board, rarely establishing a family or home. Perhaps because of their life-style, most of these artisans were men.

The fruits and flowers of their art

It is frequently illuminating, but sometimes exasperating, to attempt to classify regional characteristics through identifiable decorative motifs. Fales and Bishop warn that due to "migration, emulation, and transportation," there may be more exceptions than rules. Mrs. Pat Coblentz, assistant director of the Museum of American Folk Art believes that ready recognition comes only through exhaustive and extensive study. Nevertheless, some generalizations have been drawn by historians over the years, constituting if not strict patterns then at least loose guidelines.

Seventeenth-century craftsmen were apt to paint flat, abstracted leaf forms, simply drawn, and more or less precisely executed. In addition, scrolls,

palmettes, heraldry, and embryonic fleurs-de-lis have been identified by Fales and others as typical of the earliest decorated furniture.

The Connecticut River valley, which, as Fales and Bishop point out, was in a location to cock a watchful eye on the urban design scene but preferred to develop a style of its own, is known for favoring birds (often pheasants), scrolls, and leafy vines, in addition to the stylized tulips and roses that are the hallmarks of much decorated Connecticut furniture. The stylized sunflowers, or Tudor roses, used on these earliest pieces evolved into segmented circles. Tulips, used on earlier pieces, are not often found on later Connecticut furniture. Vines became smaller and highly stylized, progressing to simple diamonds and bull's-eyes, which in turn evolved into "colorful and well-ordered doodles."

Hudson Valley Dutch *kas* were popularly ornamented with pendant arrangements of fruit, flowers, and birds. It is believed the Dutch based their motifs on baroque carved ornament, or perhaps on aspects of baroque *trompe l'oeil* wallpaper designs.

The furniture of the Pennsylvania Germans (from 1770 to 1810 and on) is easy to spot. Its gay, pleasing, and colorful decoration is often associated with folk art. Many Pennsylvania German motifs can be traced to Near Eastern origins. The Germans who settled in the area (mistakenly referred to as Pennsylvania Dutch, a distortion of the German *Deutsch*) migrated from a country propitiously located on overland trade routes between Europe and Persia. Execution of the motifs—bold, sometimes crude, but with great spirit and color—is often stylized. The Germans depicted abundant flowers and fruits, heraldic figures and animals, angels, primitive scenic designs, and lots

Above: Examples of typical decorative motifs.

Left: Chest with drawer, Guilford-Saybrook area of Connecticut, ca 1710. Courtesy The Henry Ford Museum. The graceful symmetry of painted undulating vines arranged across the entire front panel of this chest and drawer is a typical Guilford area decoration of the period. Tulips, thistles and Tudor roses or "sunflowers," derived from European heraldic and textile designs, add detail to a structurally simple piece.

of birds—from gaily festooned peacocks to the everyday robin.

During the Federal period, which saw the classical revival of architectural elements from ancient Greece and Rome, decorators turned to wreaths, urns, swags, tablets, and busts—all hallmarks of the architectural style of the 18th century English "classical king," Robert Adam.

The brightly painted so-called American Sheraton fancy furniture (1800-1850) was inspired by the carved and inlaid decoration of the late 18th century English Sheraton style. (Not all American Sheraton furniture was painted; many fine early pieces—1794 to 1800—were carved.) Sheraton fancy furniture often featured cameo-like panels, shells, plumes, cornucopias, leaves and fruit, in addition to classic urns and swags and musical instruments such as horns, lyres or harps. It was influenced by the Adam style during its period of popularity, but then progressed to darker-colored motifs and gold striping. By the mid-19th century, fancy furniture was out of fashion.

Perhaps in competition for the popular fancy chairs, some producers of Windsor chairs between 1800 and 1825 began to widen the traditional top slat to accommodate some painted decorations. It should be noted, though, that purists do not consider these true Windsors.

Boston rockers were another popular type of hand- and stencil-decorated furniture produced throughout the 19th century and in great quantity from the 1830s onward. These rockers were both hand and stencil decorated with either simple rosettes painted at the

curved end of the crest panel or a curled leaf added to the rosette. The design might also have been either a leaf or a scroll.

Despite the unstable nature of early painted finishes, and the ruthless refinishing many pieces have undergone, experts say that it is still possible to collect prize specimens. Country pieces especially, which may be just now being dragged from the attic, are good finds, should you be so lucky as to come across one in good repair. This leads to the question of whether or not to refinish a piece with only traces of its original decoration. Ardent antiquarians admonish their students to leave an original finish the way it is. A painted motif or finish is far more valuable in its earliest state. Advises Mrs. Coblentz, "If you don't feel you can live with the piece the way it is, you probably shouldn't buy it." In the event that refinishing is desired, however, a highly skilled professional restorer is your best bet. ■

EARLY AMERICAN PAINTING TECHNIQUES

GRAINING The application of paint in well-defined brushstrokes, sometimes with a comb, or combs, or with sponges, rags, or even the fingers, to simulate the graining of wood. A lighter color normally was applied to the wood first, then the graining went on in a slightly darker tone. Graining may be coarse or fine in its execution. Folk-art pieces are often very crudely grained. If the graining is so finely done as to literally "fool the eye," then it may legitimately be called *trompe l'oeil*, as are fine painted imitations of stone, marble, tortoiseshell, and the like.

JAPANNING A technique that imitated Chinese lacquer, using paint, whiting, metal leaf, and powder. Over fine-grained woods gesso, paint, and clear varnish are applied to create the effect of decorative design—often of black or *faux* tortoiseshell—then decorated with either gold leaf applied directly to the surface or gold leaf over a gessoed, raised design.

STRIPING The application of thin painted stripes, via a striping brush or "pencil," to furniture designs.

The Neoclassic Influence

The designs of Englishmen Robert Adam, George Hepplewhite, and Thomas Sheraton had a revolutionary effect on American furniture of the Federal Period.

BY VICTORIA BRACKENWHISTLE

Many feel that the geometric delicacy of form, glowing contrasts of mahogany and satinwood, and understated inlaid ornamentation of American federal furniture distinguish the period 1785 to 1815 as the high point of American cabinetmaking. Whether or not this esthetic judgment is valid, the fact remains that American furniture of these decades found its inspiration in the English masters Sheraton and Hepplewhite, and in their mentor, Scottish architect and neoclassicist, Robert Adam.

Adam's neoclassical revival was inspired by Greco-Roman excavations at Herculaneum in 1738 and Pompeii in 1748, which reawakened Europe's interest in ancient cultures. By the mid-1760s, in both England and France, the appeal of classic forms encouraged a revolution in the decorative arts. Rococo furniture in the manner of Thomas Chippendale—and, in France, in the style of Louis XV—with its curvilinear asymmetry and exuberant carving, gave way to the chaste simplicity of a more delicately proportioned, straight-lined neoclassic style.

The new mode, known as "Louis XVI" in its French interpretation (which was popular in that country from the early 1760s), soon gained a British following, and from there spread to America, where citizens of the young Republic—the 18th-century analogue of Republican Rome—embraced it warmly.

At the forefront of this quiet revolution was Robert Adam, the second of four boys born to Edinburgh architect William Adam. Trained in his father's profession, young Adam departed Edinburgh in 1754 for a four-year period of travel and study in Italy. His expedition to the site of Emperor Diocletian's palace at Spalatro on the Dalmatian coast—rich with ornamental fragments—and his visits to ancient ruins near Rome provided inspiration for his later work in England.

The young architect returned to England in 1758 having made the acquaintance of numerous Italian painters, accompanied by artist Michelangelo Pergolesi, whose illustrated folio, *Designs for Classic Ornaments*, contributed to the vogue for neoclassic

Above: Sheraton-style armchair, possibly New York, ca 1795. In America, chairs of this type, if square-backed, were called "Sheraton"; if shield-backed, "Hepplewhite." M.&M. Karolik Collection, The Museum of Fine Arts, Boston. Right: The Etruscan Room, Osterly Park, Middlesex, England, one of the many town and country houses decorated with classical motifs by Robert Adam following his return from Italy. Photo, A.F. Kersting.

Adam's concern for decorative unity extended to the functional elements of an interior as well. In the saloon at Kedleston, Derbyshire (right) the classic urns on pedestals in the niches flanking the doorway are in fact cast iron heating units. The National Trust, London. Photo by John Bethell. Left: Adam pioneered a five-part arrangement for the service of food, as in the eating room ensemble at Osterly Park, Middlesex. The sideboard table stands between pedestals topped by urns, often used for storing and rinsing the silver plate. The National Trust, London. Photo by John Bethell. Above, left: Rams' heads decorate this gilded torchere, one of four designed by Robert Adam for the Saloon at Saltram in Devon, England. The National Trust, London. Photo by John Bethell. Above: Commode and mirror in the Princess Royal's Sitting Room, Harewood House, England. Because Adam himself was an architect-designer, he employed the finest cabinetmakers in England to translate his ideas into the wood. Thomas Chippendale, for example, created a number of Adam-designed pieces for Harewood. By permission of The Earl of Harewood; photo by A.F. Kersting.

decoration in England. (Pergolesi also lent his talent to the decoration of various Adam interiors over the next decade.)

Adam soon enjoyed the designation of "Architect to the King" and, in partnership with his brother James, attracted the patronage of England's aristocracy. The Adam brothers—or "Adelphi Adam" as they preferred to be known after 1770—designed or extensively renovated a number of important English town and country houses, including Kedleston, Sion, Osterley, Luton Hoo, Moor Park, and Culzean, among others.

In each of his commissions, Robert Adam—the creative member of the partnership—strove for total unity and harmony, coordinating all interior elements with care. Walls, windows, ceilings, mantels, door hardware, heating devices, floor coverings, and furniture were designed to complement one another in a distinctive expression of the neoclassic taste. Adam favored bright pastels for walls and ceilings. Vibrant pinks, yellows, and greens provided an effective foil for the decorative arabesques, festoons of husks, swags, urns, anthemia, paterae (small, flat, circular or oval ornaments), griffins, and other classic motifs worked in stucco or paint. Columns, pilasters, and friezes—treated with lightness and grace—ornamented many of Adam's rooms, which sometimes were decorated with classical scenes painted in medallions or compartments by his friends Antonio Zucchi, Angelica Kaufmann, Cipriani, and Pergolesi.

Though graceful, Robert Adam's furniture was chastely formal, with only serpentine or bowed fronts relieving its generally straight lines. The staunchly curved, supportive cabriole leg favored by the preceding generation of English cabinetmakers gave way to a tapering, straight, and slender leg, usually square in section, often painted or inlaid with classic motifs. Room arrangements also displayed a formal symmetry. Tall pier mirrors, surmounted by urns, festoons, and garlands were positioned between pairs of windows and anchored by straight-legged consoles. Fireplaces were flanked by sofas with straight tapering legs and by small, delicately proportioned chairs set close against the wall.

Adam gave special attention to the arrangement of dining rooms, as the social rituals of eating and drinking were integral to aristocratic life in 18th-century England. A favored five-piece arrangement included a straight-legged sideboard table between pairs of pedestals that might also function as plate warmers or cellarettes. These pedestals were topped with matching urns, sometimes outfitted as knife boxes or containers for water.

Although large stationary pieces of Adam's furniture—bookcases, for example—were sometimes made of a soft wood painted and decorated to harmonize with the wall and ceiling treatment of a specific room, mahogany and

Mahogany armchair in the Hepplewhite mode, made in England ca 1780. Metropolitan Museum of Art, Gift of Bernard M. Baruch.

costly satinwood with its rippling golden grain were extensively used as well. Marquetry—the decorative inlay of such colorful woods as tulip, amboyna, harewood (red-tinted sycamore), and holly and sometimes ivory or metal—was frequently employed on tabletops, aprons, and other flat surfaces. Classical motifs—anthemia (stylized honeysuckle forms), vases, urns, palm fronds, lyres, and oval paterae—were inlaid in satinwood or mahogany furniture. Medallions painted to correspond with ceiling decoration are also found on Adam-style furniture.

Ironically, although Robert Adam's neoclassic designs helped to eclipse the rococo style made famous by Thomas Chippendale, Chippendale himself collaborated with Adam to execute some splendidly inlaid pieces of furniture. Adam commissioned many other reputable cabinetmakers—including Samuel Norman and France and Beckwith—to work his designs "in the wood."

Without doubt, Robert Adam was the foremost tastemaker of his generation. He acknowledged this preeminence in *Works in Architecture of Robert and James Adam, Esquires* published in 1778: "We have not only met with the approbation of our employers, but even with the imitation of other artists, to such a degree as in some

measure to have brought about, in this country, a kind of revolution . . . in the decoration of the inside, an almost total change." Between 1762 and 1792, when he finished rebuilding Culzean on the craggy Scottish coast below Ayr, Adam's interiors brought the ultimate in neoclassic decorative chic to a wealthy and aristocratic few. It remained for the popularizers George Hepplewhite and Thomas Sheraton to adapt Adam's neoclassic style for production by working cabinetmakers.

In his own lifetime, George Hepplewhite was a relatively obscure cabinetmaker. He came to London in 1760 after having apprenticed with the Gillow firm of Lancaster, and carried on his trade for 24 years without attracting special notice. His reputation grew posthumously, for in 1788, two years after his death, Hepplewhite's widow, Alice, published a book of designs entitled *The Cabinet-Maker and Upholsterer's Guide* under the imprint of "A. Hepplewhite and Co."

Intended for use by cabinetmakers whose distance from London prevented their keeping abreast of the latest styles, the Hepplewhite *Guide* was emphatically practical. "In having combined near three hundred different patterns for furniture in so small a space, and of so small a price . . . we flatter ourselves that they will be found serviceable to young workmen in general, and occasionally to more experienced ones," stated the *Guide*'s preface.

Without question, the *Guide* met a need among rank and file cabinetmakers. Numerous surviving examples of period chairs and other articles of furniture, closely patterned after Hepplewhite's designs, attest to its widespread popularity in America as well as in England. In general, Hepplewhite designs are simple sturdy versions of the neoclassic style pioneered so distinctively by Robert Adam. The *Guide* provided examples of most of the fashionable furniture forms of the day—chairs, tables, and desks were designed with straight-tapering legs either round or square in section, sometimes terminating in a spade foot. Chests of drawers with straight or bowed fronts were shown with simple

high bracket—or "French" bracket—feet. Sideboard tables and pier tables had serpentine or gracefully bowed fronts in the Adam manner.

A number of illustrations of shield-back chairs resulted in Hepplewhite's being credited—erroneously—with inventing the form. He only popularized it. (Shield-backs were popular before publication of the *Guide*.) These had pierced splats centered by a characteristic swag-and-urn device or with three "Prince of Wales" feathers. The *Guide* also provided designs for up-to-the-minute square-back chairs having three or five splats carved with various motifs: feathers, swags, flaming lamps, urns, and wheat ears, the latter being especially associated with Hepplewhite.

Marquetry was suggested as appropriate decoration for the tops of tables—arabesques, swags of husks, and large foliated paterae were inlaid on tables, commodes, and on the other flat surfaces. Pier glasses, both oval and rectangular in form, were often shown with metallic gilded crests in the form of festoons, swags, and urns. Window seats with scrolled side supports, stools with tapering or saber legs, and several styles of sofa—including examples of the elegantly bowed French confidante—provided a full complement of upholstered seating pieces.

Although Hepplewhite's *Guide* offered sketches of formal sideboard tables with accompanying pairs of pedestals and urns imitating the high style of Robert Adam, it also inlcuded several more practical designs for sideboards. These had enclosed storage drawers for bottles and cutlery, eliminating the need for several extra pieces of furniture.

As Ralph Fastnedge points out in his book, *English Furniture Styles*, Hepplewhite's was a relatively small business—not even listed in the London directories. Fastnedge writes: "The designs publicized (posthumously) in the *Guide* . . . while giving a good indication as the the nature of his best and most expensive pieces, were probably representative also of the work of several of his competitors." (One such competing firm, Seddon & Sons, employed more than 400 apprentices and

Top left: English late 18th century Carlton House desk, mahogany with brass gallery. Stair and Company, New York. Top right: English secretary, ca 1780, mahogany and satinwood. The Metropolitan Museum of Art, Gift of Irwin Untermeyer. Above: Mahogany English Sheraton-style sideboard, ca 1790, encloses a chamber pot in small cupboard to the side. Courtesy Linlo House, New York.

Mindful of its philosophical antecedents in Greece and Rome, the young American republic embraced the neoclassic style.

workers and was patronized by clients from America as well as from England.)

Despite his own personal obscurity in the world of London cabinetmakers, Hepplewhite's *Guide* met an apparent need, for a second edition was brought out in 1789. Yet a third appeared in 1790, the year in which Robert Adam embarked upon the final period of his Culzean commission, and in which Thomas Sheraton—formerly a journeyman cabinetmaker—came to London.

Sheraton was born in 1751 at Stockton-on-Tees. Well into middle age, he moved to London, relinquished cabinetmaking, and set himself up as a drawing master, writer, bookseller, and Baptist lay preacher. Though his skill as a designer and draftsman was readily apparent, Sheraton lacked talent for making money. The publications from which he sought to earn a living, though popular, were too expensively produced to yield a profitable return. Thomas Sheraton's later years were sadly impoverished, and his family was left in hard circumstances following his death in 1804.

His first book of designs, *The Cabinetmaker and Upholsterer's Drawing Book*, appeared between 1791 and 1794 in four parts dealing respectively with geometry, perspective, furniture design, and ornament. A second edition was published in 1802. Sheraton intended his book to provide workable instructions for the latest styles and most fashionable ornamental designs, offering—as Hepplewhite's *Guide* had not—specific direction in "the art of making perspective drawings" and "patterns for ornaments to enrich and embellish various patterns of work."

Sheraton's conceptions clearly were influenced by the work of Robert Adam, for straight tapering legs and lightness and delicacy of form dominate his designs. His drawings of chairs

are especially distinctive. Though he illustrated several examples of the shield-back form (which was waning in popularity by the early 1790s), Sheraton preferred the straight-backed side chair which has long since become associated with his name. Typically, such chairs had three to five vertical stiles composing the back splat—carved with swags or other classic motifs—and straight tapered round legs ornamented with reeding. Fine-grained Cuban mahogany was recommended for their construction.

Although he designed fewer upholstered seating pieces than Hepplewhite, Sheraton gave close attention to small articles of furniture for the study or boudoir—fire screens, ladies' desks, work tables, dressing tables, pot cupboards, and washstands. These pieces were treated with a delicacy that revealed Sheraton's affinity for French design in the then-prevailing style of Louis XVI. (Writing in 1940, furniture historian Arthur Hayden aptly characterized Thomas Sheraton as "Louis Seize á l'Anglaise.")

While Hepplewhite preferred simple four-post canopied beds ornamented chiefly by carving, Sheraton let his imagination flow free, conceiving domed, elaborately draped and ornamented specimens including an ingenious "Summer bed in two compartments" that permitted husband and wife to slumber separately on steamy nights.

Sheraton's bemusement with mechanical novelties—dressing chests with fitted slide-out compartments, basin stands with water reservoirs, ladies' dressing chests with concealed bidets—is most apparent in his design for bedroom and library furniture. (This may reflect some influence of Thomas Sherer, whose drawings in *The Cabinetmaker's London Book of Prices* and

in the 1788 *Designs For Household Furniture* exhibited a fondness for mechanical contrivance.)

To maintain an appropriate degree of sophisticated formality with his "mechanical" furniture, Sheraton favored the tambour closure to conceal the working or utilitarian components of such pieces. (A tambour is a series of wooden, reeded elements set parallel to each other and glued to a canvas backing, allowing for extreme flexibility. Rolltop desks use this type of closure.)

He offered advice on the proper layout of drawing and dining rooms—on a less grand scale than Adam's conceptions—but properly formal, with pier mirrors above consoles or settees and a rigorous symmetry throughout. Sheraton's diningroom furniture was practical. His sideboards contained drawers and cabinets for storage as well as a decorative brass railing at the rear to keep bottles and knife boxes from sliding off.

His ornamental drawings displayed the same neoclassic decorative motifs favored by Adam: urns, swags, husks, waterleaves, and cherubic heads appear on his "pilasters for commodes," while anthemia, lyres, paterae, and medallions are found on bed pillars, cornices for friezes, and on legs for various kinds of tables. Inlaid crossbands of decoratively grained wood were much favored for large pieces of case furniture.

In *Designs for Household Furniture* "by the late T. Sheraton, cabinetmaker," published posthumously in 1812, it is apparent that Sheraton's imagination grew ever more unbridled—and his conceptions more fantastic—in his last impoverished years. The heads and feet of various beasts—lions, camels, and griffins—as well as sphinx heads and caryatids, embellish these late designs, which are closer in

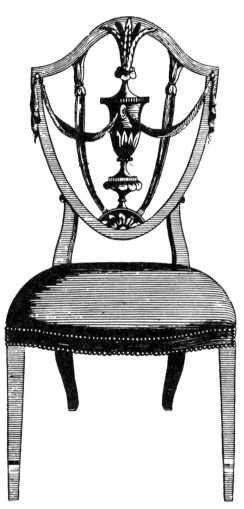

feeling to the later Empire style than to the more delicately classical Louis XVI he previously favored. Many are overly contrived and mechanically elaborate, representing a departure from earlier *Drawing Book* designs which more nearly exemplify the simple neoclassicism of Robert Adam.

It was the earlier, more simple and graceful neoclassic interpretations of Sheraton, Hepplewhite, and Adam that first caught the fancy of Americans. The young American Republic, ever mindful of its philosophical and governmental antecedents in Greece and Rome, was quick to embrace the neoclassic style (whether French articles of the Louis XVI period or English pieces in the manner of Adam, Sheraton, or Hepplewhite). In general, the so-called Federal period in American furniture-making extended approximately from 1790 to 1815, after which—like Sheraton's later designs—American furniture designs embodied a more archaeologically exact interpretation of the classic style, eventually evolving into the heavier curves of Empire design.

In federal America, the dining room assumed greater importance than before. Sideboards combining the side table and knife-box forms, inlaid with marquetry ovals and crossbanding, were in demand. Sets of side chairs—"Hepplewhite" if shield-backed and with tapering squared legs, "Sheraton" if square-backed with round, fluted tapering legs—were carved with characteristic neoclassic devices, or painted.

As in Europe, marquetry was a popular means of decoration. While inlaid classic motifs are also found on American pieces, patriotic devices such as stars or the American eagle were used widely. A great deal of American furniture of this period was painted and ornamented with landscape vignettes, musical instruments, sheaves of wheat, cornucopia, and other motifs applied in colors and in gilt. These highly decorative pieces, mostly chairs and settees, came to be known as "Sheraton fancy furniture."

As scholars point out, despite the improvements in travel and communications that fostered an overall homogeneity of furniture design in this country after 1790, some regional differences in interpreting designs are apparent. Baltimore cabinetmakers, for example, often embellished their furniture with *verre églomisé* panels (reverse paintings on glass). Some of the finest painted fancy furniture was also produced in Baltimore, where more than 50 shops were engaged in this art at the turn of the century. And Baltimore became justly famous for the quality of its delicate satinwood inlay on tables, chairs, and other pieces.

In Boston, John and Thomas Seymour produced outstanding mahogany and satinwood furniture. They popularized a unique furniture form—the tambour desk—with tambour closures extending horizontally above a folding writing flap and two drawers below. Another well-known New England name of the period is that of Samuel McIntire. An architect who also had great skill as a carver, McIntire decorated furniture—usually after the basic form had been made by another cabinetmaker—with such distinctive carved embellishments as baskets of fruit and cornucopia. Several of McIntire's pieces are identical to those illustrated by George Hepplewhite and Thomas Sheraton, attesting to the strong influence of English designers on American production. ∎

The Sheraton-style sofa, ca 1800, at the bottom of this page is attributed to Samuel McIntire of Salem, on the basis of typical carved basket of fruit at the crest and the baluster-on-urn carved armrests. The M. & M. Karolik Collection, The Museum of Fine Arts, Boston. On the page opposite, the Adam-style urn on pedestal is English, ca 1780. This delicately inlaid set is one of a pair, intended to flank a center sideboard table. Such pedestals were functional as well as decorative, often fitted with wine racks or compartments to keep food hot. The urns served as knife boxes or water containers. The Metropolitan Museum of Art, gift of Morris Loeb. Opposite page, top right: Engraved plate of chair back designs from Sheraton's *Drawing Book*, 1791-1794. New York Public Library Picture Collection. Below it is a Hepplewhite-style card table, probably made in Baltimore ca 1795. Inlaid pendant bellflowers were popular on Baltimore furniture. M. & M. Karolik Collection, The Museum of Fine Arts, Boston.

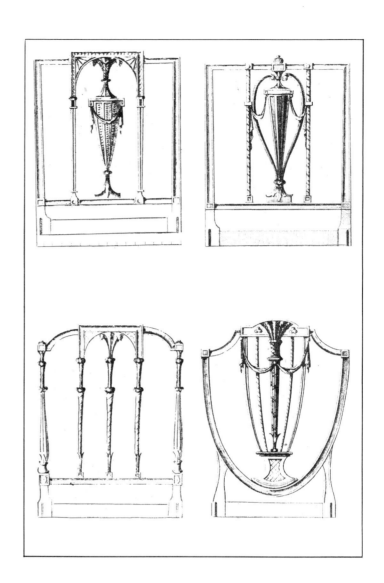

Baltimore Fancy Furniture

Hugh and John Finlay were among the most skilled of the Baltimore cabinetmakers who specialized in painted furniture during the Federal period.

BY RONALD PILLING

Baltimore equaled or surpassed older and larger cities in terms of economic growth, shipping activity, and general prosperity by 1800. To serve the needs of the moneyed merchant class, Federal-period cabinetmakers of that Patapsco River port produced graceful furniture in the Sheraton-Hepplewhite

mode. Refined Baltimore pieces of the period were known for their delicate bellflower inlay, églomise panels, and distinctive painted decoration. Brothers Hugh and John Finlay were among the many Baltimore cabinetmakers to specialize in painted or "fancy" furniture, which remained popular for 40 years.

The Finlays were born in Ireland and received their training in that country, at the time so influenced by London taste. Painted furniture was in vogue in England shortly after the American Revolution and was as acceptable as mahogany in English parlors when the Finlays were likely apprenticed to an Irish woodworker. Their earliest experiences were in the Hepplewhite tradition, and like many British furniture makers, they may have brought their

Hepplewhite pattern books with them when they embarked for the Colonies. They emigrated in the 1790s.

Arriving in Baltimore, the Finlays found a city bustling in its new wealth. By 1799 exports exceeded New York's, Philadelphia's, and Charleston's. Many the city's 25,000 inhabitants were nouveau riches merchants who purchased fancy painted furniture for their townhouses and country seats. Much as they commissioned artists to paint portraits of wives and daughters in their new silk finery, some, proud of their financial success, announced it by ordering chairs and settees decorated with paintings of their luxurious houses.

Listings in the Baltimore city directories indicate that Hugh and John Finlay were successful in their trade. Their shop moved from time to time, yet as it

Working in the Sheraton-Hepplewhite tradition cabinetmakers Hugh and John Finlay specialized in the painted or "fancy" furniture popular in Baltimore from 1800 to 1840. Opposite: The Imlay Room at Winterthur includes several pieces attributed to the Finlays among other pieces of Baltimore painted furniture, including the chair in the foreground and the one against the wall. The window seat may also be by the Finlays. Winterthur Museum, Winterthur, Delaware. Above: Detail from one of a set of 13 Finlay pieces; each of the 10 chairs is decorated with a view of a Baltimore house or public building ca 1805. The Baltimore Museum of Art.

Above: Legs are typically striped on this pier table attributed to the Finlays, 1800-1810. The musical score, flowers, and wheat were also popular motifs in their designs. Winterthur Museum. Below: This settee is part of a suite of 13 pieces purchased by John Morris in 1804. These are the only objects positively attributed to the Finlays. The Baltimore Museum of Art, gift of Lydia Howard de Roth and Nancy H. De Ford Venable and museum purchase.

grew, it always remained in the heart of the city's cabinetmaking district, Gay and Frederick streets, just blocks from the elegant brick townhouses of their merchant and shipowner customers. They always lived either above or several doors away from their shops.

This small harbor community was elbow-to-elbow with woodworkers from 1800 to 1840, Baltimore's golden period for painted furniture. Passersby knew what district they were visiting simply by smelling the varnish and newly sawed poplar and pine. In just five years—from 1805 to 1810—63

craftsmen listed in the Baltimore directory as "coachmaker," "cabinetmaker," "fancy and windsor chairmaker," "ornamental painter," or "carver and gilder" worked in an area, which now covers only 16 square blocks. In 1820, as many as 50 establishments were identified as makers of fancy furniture, indicating a specialization in gilding and painting.

The Finlays were clearly not the only painted-furniture makers in town, and though it is difficult to attribute many surviving pieces to particular makers, experts agree that the brothers

upheld the finest standards of their craft. William Voss Elder, in *Baltimore Painted Furniture, 1800–1840* (The Baltimore Museum of Art, 1972), the major work in the field, writes of the superiority of the Finlays' work: "The Finlays may well have been the chief producers of fine Baltimore Painted Furniture and were most likely imitated by their contemporary Baltimore cabinetmakers. By analyzing the decoration on the Morris set and through stylistic comparisons, many other pieces of Baltimore Painted Furniture of the early 19th century have been attributed here to the Finlays and the characteristics of their style may serve as an index to the optimum in Baltimore Painted Furniture." (The Morris set refers to an important group of extant pieces of furniture—the only ones positively attributed to the Finlays. John Morris bought the set in 1804.)

In 1795 the Library Company of Baltimore was chartered, and its first catalogue, published in 1809, revealed a selection of books that undoubtedly inspired the city's cabinetmakers. Hepplewhite's *Cabinet Maker and Upholsterer's Guide* was featured. So were Winkelman's books—*Histoire De L'art De L'antiquite, Account of Herculaneum*, and *Reflections Concerning the Imitation of the Grecian Artists in Painting and Sculpture*. Works discussing the classical modes provided guidance for the armorial designs and musical instrument groupings so popular on the fancy chairs, tables, and settees.

The Finlays appear to have absorbed some influence from Thomas Sheraton as they did from Hepplewhite, although we have no documentation regarding the extent of their familarity with Sheraton's design book *The Cabinet Dictionary*. In this volume, Sheraton presents careful instructions for preparing "varnish colours" as well as treatments for cane and rush seats. Most Finlay colors were ground in varnish, which accounts for the brothers' advertisements listing "Japanned card, pier, tea, dressing, shaving, and writing Tables. . . . All of various colours, ornamented and gilt in the most fanciful manner."

Painted furniture was not new in America when Baltimore chairmakers like the Finlays adapted it to Sheraton and Hepplewhite designs. It had been made in the Colonies from the 17th century. For example, Pennsylvania Germans embellished their dower chests and cupboards with birds and flowers, and Windsor chairs traditionally were painted black or green, sometimes with gold bands to outline the turnings. And in Connecticut, furniture typically had been painted with tulips, thistles, or Tudor roses, known as "sunflowers," since the 17th century. The Baltimore style, with its classic motifs,

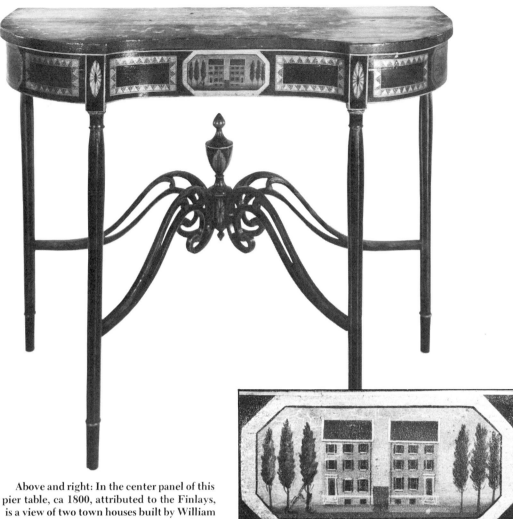

Above and right: In the center panel of this pier table, ca 1800, attributed to the Finlays, is a view of two town houses built by William Buchanan. The Baltimore Museum of Art, George G. Jenkins Fund.

was a separate but parallel development of painted furniture. Not to be confused with earlier examples, it is more in keeping with the elaborate inlays of Federal furniture from Boston or New York, made until about 1815 to 1820. *Baltimore Furniture* (1947), a catalogue of a major display of local furniture at the Baltimore Museum of Art, then directed by Adelyn D. Breeskin, explicitly notes the difference: "The carved and inlaid furniture of that period is characterized by an emphasis on elegance and decoration. The painted furniture, made by skilled craftsmen, is equally sophisticated and delicate, in no way suggesting folk art."

Furniture in the Hepplewhite style, with its slender legs and delicate features, was appropriate if all a decorator planned was some subtle striping or painted banding. In Baltimore, how-

ever, furniture decorators were more serious about their art—in fact, many did portraits and landscapes on canvas as well. They needed flat spaces for their work, so they modified the basic arrow-back Windsor–type chair. Such chairs offered the painter wide, flat top rails for major medallions. The center splat of three or five splat supports was often as wide as four inches for a second—and different—medallion. This second motif was often repeated on the broad front stretcher or the front seat rail.

These medallions were the fancy chair ornamenter's masterpieces, and the Finlay shop gave customers a wide selection of designs from which to choose. In 1804 they advertised their products as "Varnished, gilt, and ornamented in a stile not equalled on the continent—with real Views, Fancy

"The Finlays emphasize elegance and decoration"

Landscapes, Flowers, Trophies of Music, War, Husbandry, Love, & c., & c." Such designs appear on pieces attributed to the Finlays as well as to their competitors.

Perhaps the most fascinating Finlay medallions illustrate architectural views. The best preserved set of Baltimore painted furniture extant belonged to the Morris family and bears 17 polychrome views of various Baltimore public buildings and private homes on 13 pieces of furniture. Accompanying Morris-family proof-of-purchase records is a memorandum identifying the buildings. Chairs and settees are marked with corresponding numbers on the back of the seat rails. Curiously, we know of no connection between those buildings and the Morris family.

Only two of the homes illustrated on the furniture still stand, but other available material shows that portrayals on the Morris-family furniture are remarkably accurate. The manors are pictured amidst lush gardens, neatly fenced and landscaped. Details down to the white lintels, muntin strips in the many-paned windows, Chinese Chippendale porch railings, and column pediments are carefully drawn, despite the fact that each medallion is a scant 9 by 4 inches.

A set of furniture attributed to the Finlay brothers which first belonged to William Buchanan features architectural decorations on the skirts of a card and a pier table. Clearly, these were special commissions. On the central panel of the card table is the story-and-a-half Buchanan country home, with its wide porches and Federal-style entry, flanked by tall windows. The pier table features two townhouses built by Buchanan for members of his family at 17 and 19 North Gay Street in Baltimore. The Finlays' painter would only have had to look across the street for this view, for the shop was on Gay Street then, about half a block north of

the Buchanan home.

In an October 10, 1804, advertisement in the Baltimore *American and Commercial Daily Advertiser*, the Finlays informed the citizens that they could "supply them with views on their chairs and furniture which they alone could do, as they hold an exclusive right for that species of ornament." If this was true, although no legislation has been turned up to support their claim, all Baltimore painted types with architectural ornamentation could be attributed to the Irish brothers. Several pieces have been found with illustrations identical to those on the Morris set, and Baltimore scholars agree that those also are the work of the Finlays. Other examples, however, are not up to their usual standards, so either they hired additional and less talented ornamenters or, more likely, with no truth in advertising commissions to curb their enthusiasm, they stretched the facts a bit to embellish their advertisements.

The Finlays employed decorators from time to time and didn't do all the painting themselves. The practice was not unusual; for example, a competitor, Thomas S. Renshaw, used painter John Barnhart to decorate a pair of side chairs and a settee in 1815. They signed Renshaw and Barnhart on the back of the seat rail on the settee. Barnhart was not as skilled as the Finlay decorators, which is reflected in the crude gilt applications on this furniture.

We know of at least one Finlay-employed decorator—a Mr. DeBeet. In a letter to Rembrandt Peale in 1825, Thomas Jefferson apparently asked the artist's opinion of "Mr. DeBeet," who must have been a prospect for the seat of painting at Jefferson's fledgling University of Virginia. This letter has been lost, but Peale's response has been preserved at the Massachusetts Historical Society: "For a while he was engaged in Baltimore ornamenting Windsor chairs for Messrs. Finlay when I became acquainted with him and it is only of late that he has attempted to make pictures or landscapes. I cannot but think his practice on the chairs has been injurious to his taste."

"Mr. DeBeet" must certainly have been Cornelius DeBeet, a fancy painter who appears off and on in Baltimore directories. If he had been in the full-time employ of the Finlays it must have been prior to 1810, or in the period from 1813 to 1829, for at other times he is listed as a painter at different addresses. He could, of course, have worked on contract for the brothers, as he at no time calls himself a maker of chairs or cabinets. Many other craftsmen are shown as "ornamental painter," "gilder," "coach painter," or "Japanner," indicating that the furniture

Opposite: Although this corner table has been attributed to Joseph Barry, it is similar in design and decoration to documented Finlay furniture, causing some dispute in the matter of attribution, 1800–1810. Above: The important center panels on chairs like this one were painted by the Finlays; lesser decorative elements may have been done by other craftsmen. Below: Window seat attributed to the Finlays, 1800–1810. All Winterthur Museum.

129

makers probably sent some of their pieces to specialists for painting.

The Finlay brothers may have been as skilled with the brush as with the saw. John is carried in the directories for two years as a "painter" or "coach painter," just before the first mention of them as partners, in 1803. Researchers think that at least at that early date the brothers worked at the palette as much as at the lathe. John had some formal training, for the manuscript minutes of the Royal Dublin Society recorded on March 3, 1774, that "the following boys were admitted into the drawing schools—John Finlay. ... Into the school of Figure Drawing." Hugh is listed as a gifted painter by onetime trustee of the Maryland Historical Society Dr. James Bordley. His unpublished manuscript (circa 1946) is kept at the society.

Not all of the work on the Finlay furniture would have required the talents of a master like DeBeet. Besides the detailed medallions, chair legs were embellished with simple gold stripes, and rails of insufficient width for medallions often have trailing grapevines or acanthus leaves. Gilt paterae appear on the stiles of legs or back supports, and plain, sawtooth-edged panels are sometimes added to either side of the main medallion on chair-top rails and table skirts. When exotic veneers or marble were not used on table tops, the wood was often marbelized and edged with sawtooth banding.

Local woods were the standard for most painted pieces, for grain was obscured when the base color was laid on. Like others of the trade, John and Hugh Finlay used enormous amounts of pine, poplar, gumwood, and American maple to create their elegant works.

About 1820 a new painted style began to emerge, in which design was

Opposite top: The five painted panels of musical, armorial, and agricultural trophies on this card table are also found on other examples of Finlay furniture. Opposite bottom: Benjamin H. Latrobe's drawing of designs for the White House to be done by the Finlays. The classical, archaeological style exhibited here was not accepted in Baltimore until later. Right: This corner table, ca 1800, is attributed to the Finlays because of its distinctive polychrome decoration. All: The Maryland Historical Society, photos Erik Kvalsvik.

based on classical Greek and Roman archaeological models. The result bears more likeness to Duncan Phyfe's work than do earlier examples. Phyfe's brother Lachlan was employed in Baltimore as a carver from 1807 to 1808, in a shop just a block from the Finlays. He undoubtedly knew the brothers, and though there is no evidence to support it, he may have corresponded with his old Baltimore friends after he moved to New York to work for his brother. The styles in vogue in New York did make their way to Baltimore, through Lachlan Phyfe or not.

No single extant piece of this classical-revival furniture has been positively attributed to the Finlays—or any other maker. We know, however, that the Finlays stayed in the furniture business until at least the late 1830s, so we assume they adapted to the new designs. Letters in the Manuscript Collection at the Maryland Historical Society reveal that the architect Benjamin Latrobe came to the Finlays for furniture he planned in his 1809 White House remodeling. His drawings for a side chair and settee are enclosed with his correspondence to the Gay Street Shop. The designs are based on archaeological styles by Englishman Thomas Hope (author of *Household Furniture and Interior Decoration*, 1807).

Latrobe's drawings were unlike anything that had been produced in Baltimore and were representative of what became popular a decade later. Strongly Greco-Roman, the chairs have a sharply raked back and concave-curved crest rail. The settee has no back at all. The architect indicated how the painted decoration should appear as well, with classical rosettes, strings of acanthus leaves, and a medallion with a shield as its focal point on each settee arm.

None of the Finlays' correspondence with Latrobe remains, nor is there any evidence that they actually completed this furniture. Detailed drawings sent by Latrobe, however, prove that they were familiar with the style long before any of their competitors.

It is not outlandish to speculate that the Finlay's Gay Street shop produced styles in the Empire manner. Extant furniture of the era shows Finlay painting techniques and attitude. Similar rosettes, armorial motifs, and acanthus leaves appear on both Baltimore Federal and Empire furniture. Later pieces evidence skill equal to that of any gilder who might have worked for the Finlays from 1800 to 1810.

The Baltimore City Directory listings for "John and Hugh Finlay, Fancy Furniture Warehouse" cease in 1837, as tastes began to change. Factories were beginning to produce cheaper furniture in much greater quantity, and hand painting was often supplanted by stenciling. It was a brilliant four decades for the Finlays and their associates. From "painters" and "fancy chair maker" they grew to "fancy furniture manufacturers" with a "fancy furniture warehouse." In 40 years they established a reputation for craftsmanship in Baltimore the equal of that of any city in the young nation. ∎

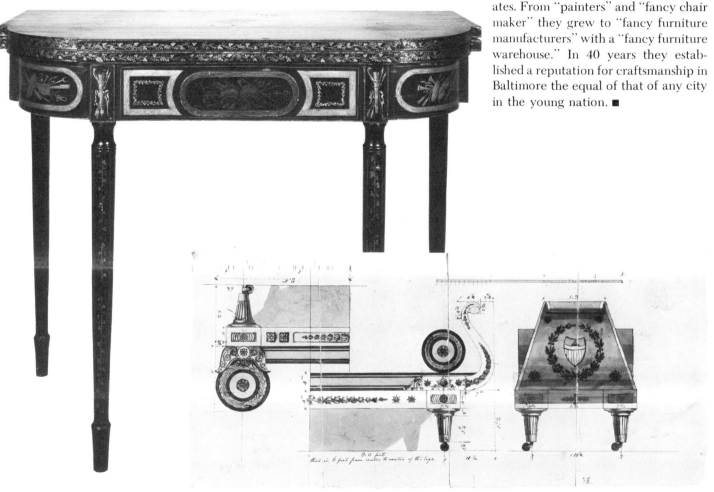

Phyfe and Lannuier: New York Cabinetmakers

Duncan Phyfe and Charles Honoré Lannuier were the best known craftsmen among a group of furniture designers who adapted the Regency and Empire styles to suit the needs of sophisticated New Yorkers.

BY RICHARD DANA REESE

At the dawn of the 19th century, New York City was a thriving center of commercial enterprise. The tradesmen who serviced her burgeoning population of 70,000 grew so numerous and diverse that in 1805–1806, for the first time, the New York Directory classified them, listing individuals as members of specific trade groups. Of cabinetmaking, the Directory's editor noted that "this curious and useful mechanical art is brought to very great perfection in this city. The furniture daily offered for sale equals in point of elegance any ever imported from Europe, and is scarcely equalled in any other city in America." Among the city's most esteemed and sophisticated furniture artisans were Duncan Phyfe, who during a major portion of his career, followed the dictates of English Regency design, and

Charles-Honoré Lannuier, who worked in both the French Empire and the Anglo-Regency styles.

Duncan Phyfe: Entrepreneur

Apart from family tradition, there is little to document the early years of Duncan Phyfe. Nancy McClelland, in her definitive study *Duncan Phyfe & The English Regency* (New York: William R. Scott, Inc., 1939), notes that he was born Duncan Fife, son of a sheepherder, in a tiny hamlet named Loch Fannich near Inverness, Scotland in 1768. With his widowed mother and siblings, he sailed for America in 1784 and ultimately settled in Albany, New York where he became apprenticed to a cabinetmaker. There, he eventually opened up his own shop on State Street as Duncan Fife, "joiner." In 1790 or 1792, he moved to New York City, setting up a workshop on Broad Street. The move evidently inspired young Fife to change the spelling of his name to something more befitting the stylish requisites of such a great city, for he is first listed in the New York Directory of 1794 as "Duncan Phyfe, Cabinet-Maker." At that time, New York City was the federal seat—a likely spot for commercial entrepreneurship—but

Congress moved to Philadelphia soon after Phyfe's arrival.

Undeterred, he settled down to business. Records show that sometime after 1800, Phyfe located on Partition Street, which ran west from Broadway to the Hudson River, and "partitioned" the populous area of the city from the wooded country to the north. There he remained for the rest of his prosperous career. Partition Street became Fulton Street—to honor the inventor of the Clermont—in 1816.

Phyfe married Rachel Lowzada in 1793 and eventually sired four sons and three daughters. As his business grew, he became a man of property, expanding his original shop to incorporate the two on either side. According to McClelland, he also purchased a residence across the street to be near his business, as was the custom of the day. He owned property in upper Manhattan—then quite countrified—and in Brooklyn. In 1837, Phyfe's two sons Michael and James were brought into the business, which became "Duncan Phyfe and Sons." Eventually, the Phyfe shop employed a hundred or more craftsmen. Among them was Duncan's brother Lauchlin Phyfe, who worked as a cabinetmaker and consummate

Below, left: Both Phyfe and Lannuier used paper labels on their furniture. These examples are from the Henry Francis du Pont Winterthur Museum. At the left, Phyfe's sketch, also from Winterthur, shows a curule chair similar to the one below, which has been attributed to Phyfe's shop 1810-1815, although substantiating documentation is lacking. Winterthur Museum.

The Lyre-backchair below is one of a set of 24 that Phyfe made for Governor William Livingston of New Jersey. Note its similarity to the chair in the sketch on the preceding page. The Metropolitan Museum of Art, gift of the family of Mr. and Mrs. Andrew Varick Stout. On the facing page is a suite of furniture Phyfe made for Samuel Foote, a New York lawyer, in 1837. The wide expanses of mahogany, the scroll supports of the bench, and the gondola-shaped chair, are all characteristic of Phyfe's work in the so-called American Empire style. The Metropolitan Museum of Art, 1966 purchase, L.E. Katzenbach Foundation gift.

carver, after having received training in Baltimore. When Michael Phyfe died in 1840, the firm name was again changed, to "Duncan Phyfe and Son."

Nancy McClelland's research shows that other members of the Phyfe clan were engaged in such New York City businesses as ivory turning and upholstery. It is believed that Duncan Phyfe apportioned out to them furniture-related contracts, when it was possible to do so. His own activities, as documented by contemporary advertisements, were diverse. In 1820, he advertised "curled hair matrasses, chair and sofa cushions." It may be surmised that he also made cases for the piano workings manufactured by one John Geib, who in 1815 announced that he could be found at Phyfe's shop.

During his long career, Phyfe made furniture for the affluent and prominent citizenry of New York, New Jersey, Philadelphia, and the South. De Witt Clinton, John Jacob Astor, William Livingston—the governor of New Jersey—and Henri Christophe, the self-styled Emperor of Haiti, were among his many customers.

Phyfe's Furniture

Chief among the many extant documented Phyfe pieces are chairs, tables, sofas, and window seats. He also made beds, sideboards, and secretaries, but few pieces of case furniture. It is important to remember that Phyfe carried on business over a period of many years, during which furniture styles changed in keeping with the dictates of current fashion. While his name has become almost synonymous with an Americanized version of English Regency styling, McClelland points out that Phyfe's career may be divided into three major stylistic periods: pre-1820, 1820–1830, and post-1830. During his earliest years, he was much influenced by English pattern books, including the *London Book of Prices*. Ernest Hagen, a New York cabinetmaker whose idio-

This square worktable with canted corners bears Phyfe's paper label with the address of 33-35 Partition Street, his workshop from 1811 to 1816. The table is strikingly similar to sarcophagus-shaped pieces in the 1805 *Supplement to the Cabinet-Maker's London Book of Prices.* On the facing page is an eagle-backed chair, ca 1815, part of a set Phyfe is thought to have made for Mayor DeWitt Clinton of New York. Museum of the City of New York, bequest of Mrs. Henry O. Tallmadge. Winterthur Museum.

syncratically spelled 1907 "Notes" on Phyfe are reproduced in McClelland's book, judged that "Duncan Phyfes chief merrit lies in the carring out and Especially improving of the 'Sheriton' style of Settees, Chairs and tables in his best period." Such pieces are characterized by delicacy of form. Chairs typically have horseshoe-shaped seats, open back panels formed of double x's that end a short distance above the seat-rail, and skillfully reeded legs. Further along in his first period, Phyfe became, in McClelland's words, a "keen advocate" of the English Regency style, particularly as it was interpreted by Thomas Hope's *Household Furniture and Interior Decoration* of 1807. (In England, the Regency style arose as a reaction to the overly decorative fussiness of the Adam period of neoclassicism. Hope's designs, in particular, formed a "transition between the Adam style and Greek Revival" that incorporated in restrained fashion such archaeological motifs and references as monopodia with lions' and griffins' heads, dog paw feet, and other such devices from the Roman aesthetic. Brass inlay and metallic mounts were frequently used on furniture of the Regency period.

In an interpretation that still stands, McClelland characterized Phyfe as the "American opposite" of Regency designer Thomas Hope. "Some of his earlier pieces show a distinct influence of Hepplewhite and Sheraton," she says, "but his finest work undoubtedly belongs to the period from 1810 onwards, by which time he was one of the leading cabinetmakers of the United States."

He also relied heavily, in his pre-1820 period, on delicately carved ornamentation which has become the hallmark of his shop. In particular, the motifs of the bowknot, thunderbolt, and the swag with tassels decorate the crest rails of many documented Phyfe sofas and chairs. His distinctive "waterleaf" motif embellishes the legs of tables and seating furniture alike, and his delicate reeding—confined, on couches, to the *fronts* of the legs—is considered a Phyfe hallmark. McClelland notes that Phyfe standardized some of his carved motifs for furniture by hanging detailed draw-

ings of favorite motifs in his shop and encouraging his carvers to use them in combinations suitable to various types of furniture, as the orders were received.

While Phyfe's shop succeeded in turning out a wholly distinctive type of furniture during this period (including his famous lyre-back and eagle-back chairs), it should be reemphasized that not all pieces with the water leaf carved and reeded "look" of the so-called American Regency were made by Phyfe or his workmen. Attributions to the Phyfe shop are generally made on the basis of labeling, documentary

evidence such as bills of sale (Phyfe's account books are not known), and quality of workmanship. Constructional details typical of the Phyfe shop include extremely fine cock-beading on the edges of drawers, delicately dovetailed joints, white wood linings of drawers, and the expert quality of the carved decoration which—in its low relief—has been likened to stone carving.

After 1820, when a more literal interpretation of archaeological classicism—influenced by the French Empire style—came into fashion, Phyfe's shop gradually turned from the restrained Regency forms to the more massive

For his wealthy American clientele, Lannuier provided furniture in the various modes of French neoclassicism, from Directoire to Restauration. The delicate mahogany pier table below, bearing Lannuier's stamp and made in 1805, has details of consular period design as illustrated in La Mésangère's *Collection de Meubles et Objets de Gout* of 1802: slender reeded legs topped by a cove with ring, a pierced brass gallery, and trumpet-shaped feet bound in brass. Winterthur Museum. To its right, a rosewood veneered pier table made about 1815, bearing remnants of Lannuier's paper label, combines elements of French Empire design—dolphin feet, swan supports,

and ormolu mounts including a central figure of Apollo drawn in his chariot by bees, the symbol of the Emperor Napoleon. The Metropolitan Museum of Art, The Friends of the American Wing Fund. Lannuier made the sleigh-shaped bed of ash, mahogany, and mahogany and amboina veneer (below) for Stephen Van Rensselaer in 1817; it bears his paper label as illustrated on the title page. Meant to be placed against a wall, the bed is ornamented on one side only with French gilt fittings in the Empire taste: griffins, winged gods, and a classical head. The dolphin feet are gilded and painted. Albany Institute of History and Art, Albany, New York.

shapes of the new mode. Furniture from this decade is typically veneered in fine mahogany and features hairy-paw or hock feet. By 1830, Phyfe's style had evolved to a fuller development of the currently fashionable pillar-and-scroll furniture, much influenced by the French Restauration styles. In his outspoken fashion, Ernest Hagen—himself a 19th-century cabinetmaker of some note—described Phyfe's post-1830 work as "the abominable heavy and Nondescrip veneered style." But this, too, was executed with characteristic Phyfe finesse, as attested by a suite of living room furniture he made for New

York lawyer Samuel A. Foote, now in the collection of The Metropolitan Museum of Art.

Toward the end of his career, according to Hagen's "Notes," Phyfe also made furniture in the carved rosewood mode, as well as in maple and black walnut. He finally retired in 1847, after many decades as New York's reigning cabinetmaker. "Phyfe cannot be truthfully called an originator of styles," Nancy McClelland wrote in 1939. "He was rather an adapter, a translator of popular ideas of the moment, with distinctly outstanding achievements in craftsmanship to his credit."

Charles-Honoré Lannuier: French Emigré

What Phyfe accomplished for the dissemination of Regency taste in early 19th-century New York had its parallel in the work of the French emigré Charles-Honoré Lannuier, who interpreted the various manifestations of French neoclassicism—from Directoire to Restauration—for America's parlors. Lorraine Waxman Pearce, who has published extensively on Lannuier and his work, notes the relationship between Charles-Honoré and his brother Nicholas-Louis-Cyrille Lannuier, an *ébéniste* of Paris in whose shop the younger man was probably trained. In keeping with the French cabinetmaking tradition, Charles-Honoré Lannuier marked his American-made furniture with a metal stamp ("H. Lannuier"), and he also used, with some frequency, a succession of paper labels. Partly as a result of these markings, it has been possible to document over 50 of his pieces.

Soon after Lannuier's arrival in New York City as a young man of 26, he took out an advertisement in the New York Evening Post for July 15, 1803 (subsequently reproduced in Rita Susswein Gottesman's *The Arts and Crafts in New York: 1801–1804*, published by The New-York Historical Society, 1965):

> Honore Lannuier, Cabinet Maker, just arrived from France, and who has worked at his trade with the most celebrated Cabinet Makers of Europe, takes the liberty of informing the public that

he makes all kinds of Furniture, Beds, Chairs, & C., in the newest and latest French fashion and that he has brought for that purpose gilt and brass frames, borders of ornaments, and handsome safe locks, as well as new patterns.

As this advertisement suggests, Lannuier's earliest documented pieces, made soon after he settled in New York City, are reminiscent of designs of the French Consulate period, published in Pierre de la Mésangère's pattern book, *Collection de Meubles et Objets de Gout*, 1802. A pier table made about 1805 and now in the collection of The Metropolitan Museum of Art, for example, has characteristic Consulate period details: flaring feet with brass fittings, reeded legs, a pierced brass gallery, and a shelf outlined in brass.

That Lannuier, like Phyfe, could also work masterfully in the prevailing New York version of the English Regency is reflected in other pieces with slender, reeded legs, dog paw feet, and water leaf or other foliate carving. It is known that at least one major New York City museum accepted a "Phyfe" piece on the basis of its fine workmanship, later to find that the table had, in fact, been crafted by Charles Honoré Lannuier and bore his stamp in an unobtrusive spot. Like Phyfe's, Lannuier's cabinetmaking skill brought a great deal of business from persons of wealth and prominence.

Lannuier is perhaps best remembered for his pieces in the French Empire style, characterized by their winged and gilded caryatid supports, and hocked animals legs, after designs in La Mésangère. In 1817, he made an elaborate sleigh-shaped bed for Stephen Van Rensselaer in the Empire taste, with painted dolphin feet and embellished with decorative French gilt mounts of griffins, winged gods, and a classical head. Firmly affixed to the bed is Lannuier's label, engraved by Samuel Maverick, enclosed within the drawing of an elegant cheval glass. It seems incongruous that the English portion of Lannuier's bilingual message is spelled phonetically, with a French accent:

> Hre. Lannuier/Cabinet Maker from Paris/Kips is Whare House of/new fashion fourniture/Broad Street, no. 60,

New York./Hre. Lannuier./Ebeniste de Paris/Tient fabrique & Magasin de Meubles/les plus a la Mode,/New-York.

The documentary record of Lannuier's business is brief, and it ends abruptly. He is first listed in the New York Directory of 1804–1805 at 60 Broad Street, and his last listing—at the same address—appears in the edition of 1819–20. In 1821, there is an entry for his widow, a resident of 36 Orchard Street. Also in the New York Directory for 1821 is a succinct—and perfectly spelled—advertisement for "John Gruez, Successor to H. Lannuier, Cabinet-Maker from Paris, Keeps his Warehouse of New-fashioned furniture at no. 60 Broad Street, New York."

The work of Phyfe and Lannuier—and of such contemporary cabinetmakers as Michael Allison and George Woodruff—assured New York City's prominence as a furniture-making center during the first quarter of the 19th century. In subsequent decades, the tradition was upheld by other cabinetmakers working in various revival styles—among them Alexander Roux, Leon Marcotte, and John Henry Belter—who, like Phyfe and Lannuier, emigrated to this country from abroad.

As tastes changed, the work of Phyfe and Lannuier was taken for granted, if not entirely forgotten. Hagen points out that some of Phyfe's descendants thought so little of their heirloom furniture that they even "threw away some hansom old Chairs." With the general resurgence of interest in American antiques during the 1920's Phyfe's water-leaf carved and reeded chairs, tables, and couches so captured the public fancy that any piece of furniture remotely resembling the style was generically designated "Phyfe." Many genuinely old pieces, of similar appearance but varying quality, were likewise erroneously attributed to his shop.

Today's scholars and collectors are more cautious in assigning attributions. But interest in Phyfe and Lannuier and other New York cabinetmakers of their generation continues unabated, and documented pieces of that period are eagerly purchased at high prices when they appear in the marketplace. ■

Shaker Chairs

Behind the creation of each piece of furniture was the principle that it should neither require too much precious time in cleaning nor, by its decoration, divert the mind from God.

BY BARBARA COEYMAN HULTS

Shakerism developed from the English Quaker tradition. In England, a group under the leadership of James and Jane Wardley broke from the Quakers in 1747 and, because of their physical enthusiasm in worship, were called Shaking Quakers. The sect became known as Shaker and finally, The United Society of Believers. For the United Society of Believers, the testimony of Christ was revealed through the visions of Ann Lee.

Ann Lee, known after her revelations as Mother Ann Lee, joined the group in 1758 at 22. Twelve years later, after much religious testimony and fervor, she became their leader. Mother Ann and members of the group were often harassed and imprisoned because they preached a doctrine that didn't conform with the teachings of the Anglican Church. During one of her imprisonments, she experienced revelations indicating that Christ's Second Coming to earth would establish a new community of Believers who would live in love and celibacy. Responding to a later revelation, she sailed to America on the *Mariah* in 1774 with eight followers. It took two years for Mother Ann and the Believers to establish the first Shaker settlement near Albany. The ingathering of new members, however, did not take place for almost five years and finally happened when Mother Ann con-

vinced a local group of "New Light" Baptists in nearby New Lebanon of her powers. They were already certain that Christ's Second Appearing was at hand.

Mother Ann's task wasn't easy. She was constantly harassed by residents of the towns and villages she visited. The goal of her preachings was to convert new members to the Shaker religion. Because conversion meant that families broke up when married people left their spouses and children to join a Shaker community, Mother Ann was unwelcome in towns and villages famil-

Opposite: Serenity pervades this interior at Hancock Shaker Village in Massachusetts. Photograph, Hank Morgan.

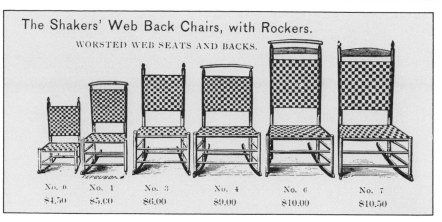

The Shakers' Web Back Chairs, with Rockers.
WORSTED WEB SEATS AND BACKS.

No. 0	No. 1	No. 3	No. 4	No. 6	No. 7
$4.50	$5.00	$6.00	$9.00	$10.00	$10.50

iar with the result of her visit. This didn't prevent Mother Ann from proselytizing across the breadth of New York and New England until her death in 1784. She taught the four principles of Shaker/Christian morality: the commitment to celibacy, true peace, a sharing of the fruits of life, and a practical equality of men and women in both secular and religious life. These four principles flowed naturally from the experience of Union in Christ. Even the early Shakers perceived of Christ as an indwelling presence, and this belief is still held today by the nine remaining Shakers.

Millennialism—belief in the end of the world and the imminent thousand-year reign of Jesus Christ—was shared by many of the utopian religious communities in 19th-century America that strove to build God's Kingdom on Earth. These sects pooled their meager resources, created laws to keep their members from backsliding and dissension, and isolated themselves from the evils of the world. As a response to the vicissitudes of persecution by the "world's people," the Shakers gathered into religious societies—11 throughout New England and more than 15 including New York, Ohio, and Kentucky. By the mid-19th century, 6,000 people were converted. They lived in 19 communities.

Shaker craft and industry

Shaken visions were practical. Through Divine Revelation Shakers caught a glimpse of Paradise to come as well as a means of creating Paradise on Earth. Shakers learned the correct way to live—in moral terms and in such mundane matters as the color to paint buildings and furniture by following the Millennial Laws and Divine Inspiration. (The laws came from Heaven as Divine Revelation in 1821.) Shaker industries were divided into two classes—those that supplied the needs of the society itself and those intended for sale to the outside world.

No matter its destination, behind the creation of each piece of furniture was the principle that it should neither require too much precious time in cleaning nor divert the mind from God by its decoration. For instance, low-backed single or double slatted dining chairs were made to be out of the way, facilitating neatness and cleanliness. They were easily slipped under the table or hooked on a peg rail against a wall.

Over a period of 40 years—to nearly the middle of the 19th century—the Shakers developed their characteristic style of chair. Low chairs had one or two back slats; ladder backs up to four. Seats were generally cane, rush, wood splint, or fabric tape known as listing. These tapes were of homespun wool, one-half to three-quarters of an inch wide, hand dyed, and webbed into the chair seat. By the mid-19th century machine-made worsted tapes were sometimes used, bought from outside the community to save time and money. Seats were often woven in two colors, such as tan and maroon, red and black or in more intricate multiple combinations. Cotton canvas webbing sub-

sequently replaced the worsted. The frame of the chair was usually constructed of maple. Birch, cherry, hickory and butternut were also used in crafting chairs. Those from Kentucky and Ohio were generally heavier in character than their eastern counterparts. In these communities, the chairs tended to have more elaborate turnings than those made in the east, reflecting a relaxed southern influence.

Tilter chairs were invented by the Shakers in 1852, when they patented the metal boot concept that allowed the chair to tilt. The metal boot was quickly abandoned for a wooden tilting ball bearing, inserted into the hollow of the chair's backpost, and held in place by a leather thong. With the new system the sitter could tilt back comfort-

ably without marring the floor or falling on his head.

Swivel stools or chairs, also called revolvers, were used in the latter part of the 19th century at school and sewing desks, tables and pianos. The shape of these chairs was influenced by the Windsor chair. (The "turned" elements of these chairs most often were in wood, but sometimes were cast in metal.) Simplicity and a light and sturdy construction followed logically from Shaker principles. Special designs were not created for their own sake; rather, regional country furniture was adapted to suit Shaker needs. The craftsmen stressed, above all, excel-

Opposite page, top: Page from Shaker catalogue ca 1860 shows chair designs from Brother Robert M. Wagan's Mt. Lebanon, New York, factory. Courtesy The Shaker Museum, Old Chatham, New York. Opposite, middle: Shaker rocker from North Union, Ohio, ca 1840. Heavier looking than chairs of New England Shaker communities, "western" pieces reflect regional influences. Courtesy Shaker Museum, Old Chatham. Opposite, bottom: Ladder back rocker, ca 1840, probably made at New Lebanon, New York. Note the "cushion rail," and the fine mushroom hand rest. Courtesy Hancock Shaker Village. Above: Children's bentwood rockers, ca 1885. Later Shaker chairs were often crafted of bentwood. Chair at right has a splint seat. At left, the seat and back are woven with tape. Courtesy Greenwillow Farm, Ltd. Right: Shaker rocker #3 from Mt. Lebanon, New York, c 1875. Inset shows the decal on the runner. The Shakers produced these chairs for sale in many sizes and styles. Courtesy Shaker Museum, Old Chatham.

Left: Slat-back curly maple chair, ca 1853. This caned chair has a patented metal tilter boot (see inset). Used experimentally, this type of boot eliminated the need for wooden ball-and-socket tilters, which tended to split with use. Courtesy Shaker Museum, Old Chatham. Opposite, top: One-slat dining chair, ca 1860. Low-backed chairs could be tucked neatly under the table after meals. The ring-turned front stretcher marks this as a relatively late piece. Photograph, Lees Studio. Courtesy the Shaker Museum, Old Chatham. Opposite, below: Child's high chair, Mt. Lebanon, 1883. This exceptionally graceful chair with mushroom-topped posts was one of six made for friends of the community. Courtesy Shaker Museum, Old Chatham.

lence in workmanship that applied to every single object they made, no matter how humble its function.

Cheerfulness was a real part of Shaker life. Although in effect a Protestant monastic order, Shakers could and did enliven their surroundings through color. Some chairs were painted and, especially from the middle of the 19th century, brightly colored tapes were woven to make chair backs and seats. (Colors had conservative names, however—"Meetinghouse blue," "Ministry green," and "Trustee brown." Each color suggested its use within the Shaker community. All pieces used by and for the ministry, for example, were likely to be painted a characteristic green.)

Only when it detracted from God's purpose was beauty frowned on. When it came as a result of fine workmanship, it was prized. For the Shakers, perfection was the goal, craftsmanship was the means, and beauty was often the result, albeit an inadvertent one.

Because most Shaker furniture at first was made to be used in the community, modifications for specific needs of individuals influenced construction: chairs, for example, could be made high or low to suit a specific purpose. Many of these community pieces were purchased by collectors as the communities disbanded. Many community pieces have been acquired by museums and other repositories. Only a small portion of the vast array of furniture made for the community has ever been found at auction.

Shaker chairs

The history of the Shaker movement is strikingly reflected in the chairs they

Clean-lined, superbly functional furniture reflected the Shaker belief that each man-made object should be "perfect unto itself".

made. The late Edward Deming Andrews and Faith Andrews, two of the most prominent Shaker scholars, write that Shaker chairs are fine examples of the precept that objects should be made "by order and use." The first rockers, writes Andrews in *Fruits of the Shaker Tree of Life* "were made for the comfort of the aged and infirm, for whom there was always the most solicitous concern. High-seated counter chairs for ironing or tailoring, revolving chairs or stools—known as swivel seats—loom stools, slipper chairs, chairs adapted to the physique of given individuals all express the intimate coordination between the craftsmanship of the sect and its cultural, religious, and economic background."

Of the different types of furniture, some consider the chair to be the most essential form. They were straight and simple in the early years, then slightly curved. Later, some became indistinguishable from other products of late Victorian design. The Believers were "pioneers" of the American chair industry. Records show their first commercial sale took place as early as 1789.

The earliest Shaker chairs are identified with difficulty, because they are so similar to the simple, painted slat back country pieces produced in the regions in which the communities were located. As the Shakers' chairmaking expertise increased, their chairs became lighter and sleeker. Frames were pared down but were very strong. (Enfield, New Hampshire, side chairs—considered by many to be the most elegant Shaker chairs—weighed from five to eight pounds.) Rockers were used in all the Shaker communities, although their use did not go without protest from many orthodox members who deplored

their rocking feature as a "seeking after ease."

The earliest rockers were often adapted from a regular chair by fitting rocker rails into slots cut into the posts. The rocker rails were short and narrow, not extending beyond the front chair posts and projecting only five to seven inches in the rear. Because of the abrupt termination of the front rockers, these chairs spilled many an enthusiastic Believer to the ground, earning the chairs the title, "suicide rockers." Cradle or sled-shaped rockers were also used on early chairs.

Rocking chairs generally had three to four slats between the back posts. Below the seat they had a rung at the rear and two rungs at the front and sides. Arm rests tended to be low, as were the seats. The comparatively narrow back posts, terminating in "acorn" finials or turned "cushion" rails, became the visual focus of the chair. (Cushion rails were made to accommodate back rests fashioned of plush [a cotton velvet] and attached to the chair by a ribbon.)

Later, rockers were especially contoured for the shape of the body to give maximum comfort and support. Slat-back rockers, with or without arms, were produced in great numbers through the last quarter of the 19th century. Some versions of the rocking chair had backs that were either woven with tape or upholstered in plush. Wooden footstools, sometimes covered with plush, often accompanied the rocker. Rocking chairs made for distribution outside the community, called "world rockers" by some, were made by the chair factory in New Lebanon, New York, until the business folded in 1935.

The New Lebanon industry

While chairs were made in all of the Shaker colonies, New Lebanon, New York, was a major center for chair construction. The industry, which began there in the late 1780s, supplied many Shaker communities with chairs. At first, rocking and side chairs were distributed principally by one-horse wagons which took the Shaker "pedlars" to the neighboring communities of Troy, Hudson, Poughkeepsie, and even far-off Boston and New York City.

About 1852, the business was reorganized by the Second and South families of New Lebanon. By 1863, the chair business was in full swing under the guidance of Elder Robert M. Wagan of the South family, whose company bore his name. A gold transfer trademark was developed to identify Shaker pieces and protect the Society from imitations. Under Wagan's direction, descriptive catalogues were printed listing prices and styles of the straight and rocking chairs made at New Lebanon. In one late 19th-century Wagan catalogue, Shaker rockers sold for between $3.50 and $17. (Today such rockers often bring $300 to $400 each.) By the 1870s, chairs became standardized, reaching the market in numbered sizes. Rockers, sold across the country in sizes zero to seven, accommodated just about everyone from infant to adult. Such chairs were marketed through the widely distributed New Lebanon catalogue, building a demand for Shaker furniture. A catalogue produced in conjunction with the 1876 Philadelphia Centennial Exposition—complete with religious propaganda—was seen by masses of people who visited the great fair.

By the mid-19th century, along with the chairs, an amazing variety of Shaker items were sold to the "world" by the New Lebanon community. Goods ranged from spinning wheels, nests of oval boxes, garden seeds, leather gloves and skins to brooms, wire and hair sieves, and sewing items.

In spite of the variety of businesses and crafts provided by each Shaker community—Shakers even had a wholesale medicinal business—the call of big business and city life tempted thousands of Shakers away from their simple life during the Industrial Revolution. By the turn of the 19th century, the Shakers counted fewer than 2,000 members.

At the newly restored Shaker community at Hancock, Massachusetts, near New Lebanon, New York, curator June Sprigg is often asked how to identify a genuine Shaker piece. "There is no easy way to tell. Even experts get fooled," she says. "There is no substitute for acquiring background knowledge. Know what the Shakers made. Learn something about wood and how it ages. Learn what kinds of techniques Shaker craftsmen employed. Many museums offer examples of Shaker furniture. There are places such as this village and the Shaker Museum in Old Chatham, New York, where Shaker furniture can be studied and books on Shaker life are available. There are no shortcuts."

At the Greenwillow Farm Shaker Gallery in Chatham, New York, Ed Pawling, a dealer, concurs. "Some people think anything simple is Shaker, and that's far from true. The Shakers had their own innovative way of doing things. It's true, though, that even ex-

Opposite page, top: Swivel chair or "revolver," maple and oak, 1850-75. Attributed to the Shakers of Enfield, New Hampshire, such revolvers were used in offices and schools. Their back splints were wood or cast metal. Courtesy Hancock Shaker Village. Opposite, below: Ironing chair, Canterbury, New Hampshire. This chair is a good example of functionalism in Shaker design. The high seat and absence of arms permit total freedom of movement at working level. Courtesy Shaker Museum, Old Chatham. Above and left: Views of a slat-back Shaker side chair with "tilters" on the rear legs, 1840's. Side chairs often had three slats. Seats were caned or woven with splints or tape. Inset (below): Wooden tilter mechanism similar to the ones used on the chair, left. Such "Tilters" permitted the chair foot to remain flat on the floor when the chair was tilted back, reducing rug and floor damage. A "tilter" is a moveable wooden ball held in its socket joint by a rawhide thong passed through the leg of the chair and pinned. Courtesy Shaker Museum, Old Chatham.

perts can be fooled and, worst of all, succumb to what is called 'Hopeful Shaker,' resulting from the shortage of good, authentic material. The best insurance a prospective buyer can have is buying from a dealer with a good reputation. A reputable dealer will give a carefully worded receipt that indicates that the piece was made by the Shakers, its provenance, and any other information he may possess. If it should happen that the item turns out to be not as represented, then the purchase price should be refunded no matter how much time has elapsed."

Shaker reproductions are to be found throughout the country, and may or may not be clearly marked. Some reproductions carry tradenames such as North Family Joiners, Shaker Workshops, and The Guild of Shaker Crafts.

It could not have been better said than by the Andrews in their book *Religion in Wood:* "The craftsmanship of the Shakers was an integral part of the life and thought of a consecrated folk. They did not think of the work of their hands—in building, in joinery, in industrial pursuits of every kind—as an art . . . but rather as the right way of sustaining their church order, the ideal of a better society. For them, the machine or tool was a servant force. It was the *purpose* of work which was important. This led to a manner of work, which in turn gave a common character—an integrity, a harmony, a subtle but identifiable quality to all the labor of their hands." Thus, it may be impossible to achieve a true Shaker reproduction, for a Shaker chair surely embodies the simple mysticism of Mother Ann's most quoted words, "Hands to work and hearts to God." ■

Fireplace Furniture

Glowing as brightly as the burning logs they secured, decorative brass andirons reflected the changing furniture styles of the 18th century.

BY HENRY KAUFFMAN

Fireplaces and andirons were central features of all important rooms in American houses built before 1830. A necessity for cooking and heating, they were not only designed for utility, but also styled for consistency with the architecture and furnishings of the times.

Kitchen fireplaces were furnished with one or more pairs of andirons to support the log fire and to arrange cooking equipment in relation to the hot coals. A jack was generally used in a large fireplace for turning a roasting spit, a necessity for evenly cooked meat. But because most kitchen andirons were made of wrought iron, they will not be discussed in this survey, which will focus on brass andirons of the 18th century.

Most types of fireplace equipment have been generally identified, but little research into the origin and dating of these accessories has been done. Stylistic features and regional characteristics have been confused, and dating has been too broad—and often too early—for andirons and other parlor fireplace equipment. Other fallacies have prevailed, particularly the belief that much fireplace equipment and most andirons were imported from England or the continent. There is ample evidence that from very early times, fireplace equipment was designed and manufactured in the American colonies. Though old newspaper advertisements carry lists of imported hardware items from England and the continent, virtually no fireplace equipment is ever mentioned in these lists. On the other hand a number of 18th-century advertisements of American-made objects such as firebacks, fenders, tongs, and bellows have been found. For example, the *Providence Gazette* of December 22, 1763 carried this commercial insertion:

DANIEL JACKSON
Founder from Boston.
Informs the public that he hath set up his Business in Providence, on the west side of the great bridge, near Capt. George Jackson's where he does all sorts of work in the Founders Trade, after the newest fashions, and in the most curious and elegant Taste: Particularly Brass Andirons, Fire shovels, Tongs, Candlesticks, Snuffers, Knockers, and all sorts of Furniture and Trimmings for Cabinet makers, Saddlers, and Chaise makers; with a great variety of other Articles, too many to be particularly enumerated. Ready money will be given at his shop for old Brass and Copper.

Other evidence for the production of brass andirons in America is provided by William Zane's advertisement in the *Pennsylvania Gazette*, November 10, 1792. The listing tells that he has imported "a general assortment of ironmongery, cutlery, saddlery, etc." The final paragraph of Zane's ad, headed AMERICAN MANUFACTURE, mentions "copper and iron tea kettles, traces, bedcords, sash cords . . . and a great variety of brass andirons, brass head and common variety."

The scarcity of English brass andirons in America can easily be explained. As early as 1650, coal and peat had largely replaced wood in English fireplaces, and by 1700 the use of coal-

Top: Billhead of New York brass founder John Bailey, for a pair of "End Irons." The andirons depicted on this bill are similar to the tall Federal pair on the last two pages of this article. Henry Francis du Pont Winterthur Museum, Joseph Downs Manuscript Collection. Above: Detail from engraved brass andiron attributed to James Wittingham, New York, ca 1770-1790. Note the solder line uniting the two halves of the hollow-cast column, indicating its 18th-century origin. Courtesy Israel Sack, New York.

This exceptionally large brass andiron stands 19½" high, 13½" wide, and 21" deep. Its size, proportion and detail reflect the sophistication and elegance of craftsmanship achieved by late 18th-century brass founders. The engraving on the plinth, urn, and finial is as competent and beautiful as that on the finest Federal silver; the concave molded and beaded elements adjoining the base of the plinth are characteristic of Philadelphia andirons, ca 1770-1790. Courtesy Israel Sack, Inc.

149

burning grates—rather than andirons to hold logs—was universal. Strangely enough, some of these grates were shipped to America at an early date, and newspaper advertisements in the big cities of the Eastern Seaboard, like Philadelphia and Boston, offer "Newcastle Coal" and "coals." But America was a land of endless forest. Wood was so plentiful that timber products were shipped abroad, and wood remained the domestic fuel of choice until well into the 19th century.

It will never be known precisely when the first andirons were made in the American colonies. However, the style and construction of the earliest surviving examples suggest that they were first made in New England in the late 17th century or the early 18th century. Chilly New England, rather than temperate Virginia, was the logical place for such early production, and in fact most of the earliest examples of brass andirons have been found there.

These early andirons are simply constructed of three pieces of metal: two of iron and one of brass. The major part is an upright column of iron, split at the bottom and spread outward to form a base or legs. A hole is punched in this column about four inches above the hearth and a rounded end of the billet bar—the horizontal connecting rod that supports the logs—is inserted and riveted into the front side. Billet bars were always made of iron, the only metal able to withstand the constant heat of the fire. Even iron shows signs of deterioration after many years of use. The top end of the column is forged into a small tenon, possibly one-quarter inch in width, which extends through the brass head and is riveted on the top. (Riveting is a simple way of joining two pieces of metal.)

Andirons, being made primarily of iron, were first manufactured by the blacksmiths whose shops were located near the center of every colonial village. Before brass foundries were operating in America, the decorative brass heads for these village-made andirons were probably imported; but by

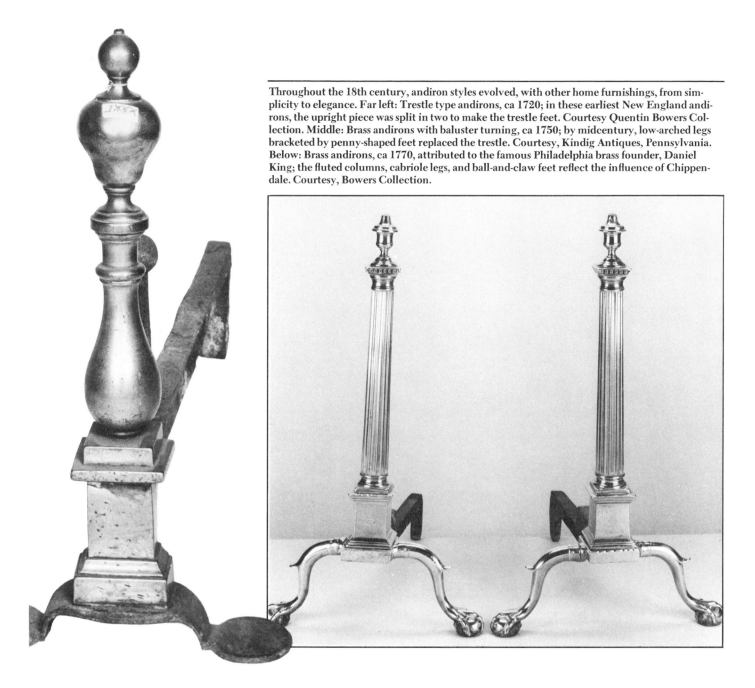

Throughout the 18th century, andiron styles evolved, with other home furnishings, from simplicity to elegance. Far left: Trestle type andirons, ca 1720; in these earliest New England andirons, the upright piece was split in two to make the trestle feet. Courtesy Quentin Bowers Collection. Middle: Brass andirons with baluster turning, ca 1750; by midcentury, low-arched legs bracketed by penny-shaped feet replaced the trestle. Courtesy, Kindig Antiques, Pennsylvania. Below: Brass andirons, ca 1770, attributed to the famous Philadelphia brass founder, Daniel King; the fluted columns, cabriole legs, and ball-and-claw feet reflect the influence of Chippendale. Courtesy, Bowers Collection.

1750 Philip Syng, a brass founder at Annapolis, was supplying "Heads or Knobs of all sizes for shovels, dogs, etc."

Some attention should be given to the style of these early andirons. They had feet that lay flat on the hearth, of the trestle type commonly found on furniture of the Pilgrim century. However, this type of andiron was inconvenient: a piece of debris lodged under one leg would tilt it precariously. Trestle-type andirons were short—possibly two feet high—and were suited for use in a bedchamber or sitting room. Larger ones with spit hooks on the front or back of the column were designed for use in the kitchen.

In the first half of the 18th century the trestle form was discarded and a separate piece of iron was attached to the bottom end of the column to form a low arch bracketed by feet shaped like pennies. This arrangement permitted only the feet of the andiron to rest on the hearth, and clearance from debris was provided between the feet. This change improved both the appearance and function of the andirons made from then on.

An important decorative feature was simultaneously introduced—the baluster column. Examples of this new form survive in both iron and brass. The baluster design was borrowed from furniture and architecture of the period, and therefore, like the earlier trestle-type examples, harmonized well with its surroundings.

With the introduction of the cast brass baluster column, the method of production changed; andirons were now made in brass foundries. The rounded upright baluster-shaped column was formed of two identical halves, hollow cast. In this procedure, the molten brass was poured into flasks (boxes) filled with damp sand, which had been impressed with a wooden pattern to leave a cavity of the desired shape.

The hollow, rounded halves of the column were united with a high-temperature solder called spelter, then the surface was smoothed on a lathe. The

line of solder appears as an andiron ages, becoming slightly oxidized, and its presence is an important clue in the identification of old andirons. (The 19th-century method of core casting permitted hollow andirons to be made in one piece; they have no telltale line of solder.)

By the middle of the 18th century there were great changes in American residential architecture and in furniture design. Merchants, traders and plantation owners acquired enough wealth to build large, gracious houses. Such elegant homes had many rooms, each one with a fireplace; sometimes there were additional fireplaces in the attic and basement. Paneling was often used on the fireplace wall, while the

other walls were plastered. Bolection moldings surrounded the fireplace; in many cases the forehearth was a marble slab. Extravagant furnishings filled these habitations and a demand for more decoratively sophisticated andirons became evident. The spell of Chippendale fell not only on furniture, but also on andirons. The baluster form was greatly refined by the addition of cabriole legs with ball-and-claw feet. Square or round fluted columns often replaced the baluster itself. Eventually the baluster column was spiral twisted and topped with a diamond-and-flame head. (Although such andirons are usually called "Revere-type," this is a misnomer; they were first made long before Revere's time.) The spiraled or

fluted columns, cabriole legs, and ball-and-claw feet of Chippendale andirons echoed the design of tea tables of the period. All seemed to be in perfect harmony.

Fine brass andirons were highly valued in the 18th century as an important item of personal property. For example, records show that in 1770, John Cadwalader paid Daniel King, a Philadelphia brass founder, £25 for a pair of andirons—a considerable sum of money for that period. (A pair of signed King andirons in the collection of the Winterthur Museum are possibly the very one made for Cadwalader.) At the same time he purchased the andirons, Cadwalader paid Philadelphia cabinetmaker Thomas Affleck £25 for his

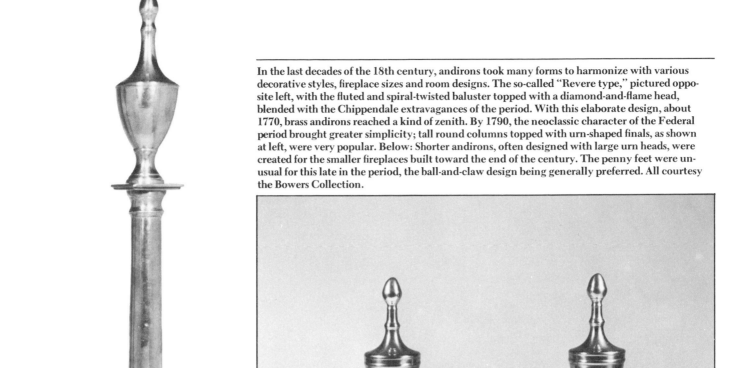

In the last decades of the 18th century, andirons took many forms to harmonize with various decorative styles, fireplace sizes and room designs. The so-called "Revere type," pictured opposite left, with the fluted and spiral-twisted baluster topped with a diamond-and-flame head, blended with the Chippendale extravagances of the period. With this elaborate design, about 1770, brass andirons reached a kind of zenith. By 1790, the neoclassic character of the Federal period brought greater simplicity; tall round columns topped with urn-shaped finials, as shown at left, were very popular. Below: Shorter andirons, often designed with large urn heads, were created for the smaller fireplaces built toward the end of the century. The penny feet were unusual for this late in the period, the ball-and-claw design being generally preferred. All courtesy the Bowers Collection.

sofa, and Charles Wilson Peale the same amount for a portrait of the Cadwalader family. Clearly, andirons were objects of high regard in this particular household.

In the late 18th century, the neoclassic character of Federal period design popularized furnishings and architecture more delicately scaled than those of the preceding Chippendale era. Fireplace jambs were ornamented with flat and round columns, inspired by ancient prototypes. The tall, round columns of the andirons shown on the billhead of John Bailey, a New York brass founder, reflect this influence. Often, Federal period andirons are topped with urn-shaped finials which are also found on other examples of

decorative art of the period. However, although the columns and heads of Federal period andirons bore the impress of neoclassic design, the cabriole leg and ball-and-claw foot remained popular until the very end of the 18th century.

In addition to the tall cylindrical andirons with urn-shaped heads or finials, a shorter type, well suited to the smaller fireplaces being installed in houses at the end of the 18th century, gained in popularity. These had large urn heads to compensate for the lack of a long column. Both the tall and the short Federal period andirons were cast in halves and joined with spelter, as the earlier 18th-century types had been. The supporting parts of the andiron continued to be joined by an iron rod to

which the head was threaded so that the andiron could be disassembled if necessary. Rods with threaded ends date from the late 18th century, when threading facilities became a common part of the metalworker's tool chest. Some andirons with penny feet were made at this time, together with the more common ball-and-claw type.

By the end of the century the elegant, tall-columned type of andiron was hard to find. A great number of short models, bearing their maker's names, appeared in New York and Boston. They reflected the fact that fireplaces had become smaller, and andirons had to be reduced in height in order to accommodate these new dimensions. ■

Selected Bibliography

Andrews, Edward Deming and Faith. *Religion in Wood: A Book of Shaker Furniture.* Bloomington and London: Indiana University Press, 1966.

Baltimore Museum of Art. *Baltimore Furniture: The Work of Baltimore and Annapolis Cabinetmakers from 1760 to 1810.* Baltimore: The Baltimore Museum of Art, 1947.

Bishop, Robert. *American Furniture, 1620–1720.* Dearborn: The Edison Institute, 1975.

— — —. *Centuries and Styles of the American Chair.* New York: E. P. Dutton, 1972.

Bridenbaugh, Carl. *The Colonial Craftsman.* New York: New York University Press, 1950.

Burton, E. Milby. *Charleston Furniture, 1700–1825.* Charleston: The Charleston Museum, 1955.

— — —. *Thomas Elfe, Charleston Cabinetmaker.* Charleston: The Charleston Museum, 1952.

Butler, Joseph T. *American Antiques, 1800–1900.* New York: Odyssey Press, 1965.

Campbell, Christopher M. *American Chippendale Furniture, 1755–1790.* Dearborn: The Edison Institute, 1975.

Carpenter, Ralph E., Jr. *The Arts and Crafts of Newport, Rhode Island, 1640–1820.* Newport: Preservation Society of Newport County, 1954.

Chippendale, Thomas. *The Gentleman & Cabinet-Maker's Director.* 3rd ed. London: privately printed, 1762. Reprint. New York: Dover Publications, 1966.

Comstock, Helen, ed. *The Concise Encyclopedia of American Antiques.* 2 vols. London: The Connoisseur, 1958.

Cooper, Wendy A. *In Praise of America.* New York: Alfred A. Knopf, 1980.

Davidson, Marshall B. *The Bantam Illustrated Guide to Early American Furniture.* New York: Bantam Books, 1980.

Downs, Joseph. *American Furniture in the Henry Francis du Pont Winterthur Museum: Queen Anne and Chippendale Periods.* New York: Macmillan, 1952.

Elder, William Voss III. *Baltimore Painted Furniture, 1800–1840.* Baltimore: The Baltimore Museum of Art, 1972.

Fabian, Monroe H. *The Pennsylvania-German Decorated Chest.* Clinton, New Jersey: Main Street Press, 1978.

Failey, Dean F., et al. *Long Island Is My Nation: The Decorative Arts & Craftsmen, 1640–1830*. Setauket, New York: Society for the Preservation of Long Island Antiquities, 1976.

Fairbanks, Jonathan L. and Bates, Elizabeth B. *American Furniture: 1620 to the Present*. New York: Richard Marek Publishers, 1981.

Fales, Dean A., Jr. *American Painted Furniture, 1660–1880*. New York: E. P. Dutton, 1972.

Fitzgerald, Oscar: *Three Centuries of American Furniture*. Englewood Cliffs, New Jersey: Prentice-Hall, 1981.

Hepplewhite, George. *The Cabinet-Maker & Upholsterer's Guide*. 3rd ed. London: I. & J. Taylor, 1794. Reprint. New York: Dover Publications, 1969.

Horner, William Macpherson, Jr. *Blue Book Philadelphia Furniture, William Penn to George Washington*. Philadelphia: privately printed, 1935. Reprint. Washington, D.C.: Highland House Publishers, 1977.

Horton, Frank L. *The Museum of Early Southern Decorative Arts: A Collection of Southern Furniture, Paintings, Ceramics, Textiles, and Metalware*. Winston-Salem: Old Salem, Inc., 1979.

Hummel, Charles F. *A Winterthur Guide to American Chippendale Furniture: Middle Atlantic and Southern Colonies*. New York: Crown Publishers, 1976.

– – –. *With Hammer in Hand: The Dominy Craftsmen of East Hampton, New York*. Charlottesville: The University Press of Virginia, 1968.

Kane, Patricia E. *Furniture of the New Haven Colony— Seventeenth-Century Style*. New Haven: New Haven Colony Historical Society, 1973.

Kebebian, Paul B. and Lipke, William C., eds. *Tools and Technologies: America's Wooden Age*. Burlington: Robert Hull Fleming Museum, University of Vermont, 1979.

Kenney, John Tarrant. *The Hitchcock Chair*. New York: Clarkson N. Potter, 1971.

Ketchum, William C. *The Knopf Collectors' Guides to American Antiques: Chests, Cupboards, Desks & Other Pieces*. New York: Alfred A. Knopf, 1982.

Kirk, John T. *American Chairs: Queen Anne and Chippendale*. New York: Alfred A. Knopf, 1972.

McClelland, Nancy. *Duncan Phyfe and the English Regency, 1795–1830*. New York: William R. Scott, 1939. Reprint. New York: Dover Publications, 1980.

Mayhew, Edgar deN., and Myers, Minor, Jr. *A Documentary History of American Interiors*. New York: Charles Scribner's Sons, 1980.

Miller, V. Isabelle. *Furniture by New York Cabinetmakers, 1650–1860*. New York: Museum of the City of New York, 1956.

Montgomery, Charles F. *American Furniture: The Federal Period, in the Henry Francis du Pont Winterthur Museum*. New York: Viking Press, 1966.

Myers, Minor, Jr., and Mayhew, Edgar deN. *New London County Furniture, 1640–1840*. New London, Connecticut: The Lyman Allyn Museum, 1974.

Nutting, Wallace. *Furniture Treasury*. 3 vols. Framingham, Massachusetts: Old America Company, 1928–33.

Parsons, Charles S. *The Dunlaps and Their Furniture*. Manchester, New Hampshire: The Currier Gallery of Art, 1970.

Sack, Albert. *Fine Points of Furniture, Early American*. New York: Crown Publishers, 1950.

Schiffer, Nancy and Herbert. *Woods We Live With: A Guide to the Identification of Wood in the Home*. Exton, Pennsylvania: Schiffer Publishing Ltd., 1977.

Schwartz, Marvin. *The Knopf Collectors' Guides to American Antiques: Chairs, Tables, Sofas & Beds*. New York: Alfred A. Knopf, 1982.

Shea, John G. *The American Shakers and Their Furniture, With Measured Drawings of Museum Classics*. New York: Van Nostrand Reinhold, 1971.

Sprigg, June. *By Shaker Hands: The Art and the World of the Shakers*. New York: Alfred A. Knopf, 1975.

Tracy, Berry B., et al. *19th-Century America: Furniture and Other Decorative Arts*. New York: The Metropolitan Museum of Art, 1970.

Whitehall, Walter Muir, et al, ed. *Boston Furniture of the 18th Century*. Boston: Colonial Society of Massachusetts, 1974.

Index

About the Authors

VICTORIA BRACKENWHISTLE, once a curator, devotes her time to writing and research on furniture.

JOSEPH T. BUTLER, Curator and Director of Collections at Sleepy Hollow Restorations, has contributed articles to every antiques publication. Former American editor of *Connoisseur*, he is author of *American Antiques, 1800–1900* (Odyssey Press, 1965).

WENDY COOPER, an assistant curator at the Boston Museum of Fine Arts, is the author of *In Praise of America* (Knopf, 1981), among other works on American furniture.

RUTH MILLER FITZGIBBONS is former editor of *American Home*, and a frequent writer on American design.

HENRY D. GREEN, a Sea Island, Georgia collector of southern furniture, writes and consults extensively on this topic. He has organized museum exhibitions in Atlanta and Athens Georgia.

BARBARA COEYMAN HULTS has specialized in writing about Shaker arts.

KATHLEEN EAGEN JOHNSON, a furniture specialist on the curatorial staff of Sleepy Hollow Restorations, Tarrytown, New York, writes frequently for decorating arts publications.

HENRY KAUFFMAN of Lancaster, Pennsylvania is the author of seventeen books and many more articles on early American antiques.

BETSY KENT, of Williamsburg, Virginia is a decorative arts specialist whose articles appear often in such magazines as *Antiques*.

MARILYN S. MELCHOR co-organized the Chrysler Museum's exhibition on Raised Panel Furniture of the Eastern Shore of Virginia, and co-authored the definitive catalogue that accompanied the show.

MINOR MYERS, JR., a historian of the decorative arts, lives in Connecticut. He is co-author of *New London Country Furniture*. (Lyman Allen Museum, 1974) and *A Documentary History of American Interiors* (Charles Scribners Sons, 1980).

RONALD PILLING, a Baltimore furniture collector and a restorationist, is a frequent contributor to many antiques publications.

RICHARD DANA REESE, a former curator of American history and decorative arts, writes and lectures frequently on American antiques.

MARVIN D. SCHWARTZ, a staff member at the Metropolitan Museum of Art, is former curator of decorative arts at the Brooklyn Museum. He is author of many books including Knopf's *Collector's Guide to Chairs, Tables, Sofas and Beds* (1982).

ROBERT TRENT, co-organizer of the Boston Museum of Fine Arts' "New England Begins" exhibition and co-author of the accompanying catalogue, is Curator of the Connecticut Historical Society.